TRUE EVIL
NEVER DIES

Jim Ochwatt

Dedication

This Publication is dedicated to the teaching's and memory of my Father & those that put other's before them self's so that humanity could have a example of what was right in the world.

The writing's and topic's covered in this book are actual / factual. It was not put together for any kind of theatrical effect. The mentioned information should be used by anyone that has a conscious , and or is effected by the problematic issue's that are covered.

I am most concerned with my grand children , and that they are not getting anything close to what I did out of life , and that when I look at what's happening in the world and how they will be effected, it makes me intimidated to the point of having to say and do something about it.

 People of the world must stand up and not fear the intimidations of corrupt leader's and or tyrant's. If they have nothing to rule, by the people not excepting there rule they will be out of the extortion business.

The definition of hierarchy must change , it can no longer have its standard set by how much money and power someone has, but instead a return to a sub culture , that need's to prevail as a mainstream culture , that is based on fairness , peace, and trust.

There has not been that many examples of how to achieve such thing's , the only real collection of figures come from thru out history's recording of them , and that they were spread out over time for the most part. People should truly honor such notable contributors of humanity by demonstrating with action's not just talk. If such action's do not take place their will be no perpetuation of integrity and the world will suffer from its own lack of self worth.

I have personally interacted with people that were kind enough to educate me even though there own life had suffered , from not accomplishing there dreams and goal's , and that they had no bitterness towards helping others to try and accomplish there's. They were the best in what people had to offer one another and I will not forget them as long as I live.

About the Author

It has always been my passion to show the transparency and disinformation that is what any government is really about. It is the object of True Evil to Explain and describe
who and how the worlds society's are manipulated by power and money. I feel for many reason's that if we as a race of human beings are to survive we must deal with this un-equality.

I cover the subjects and material in this writing from my own personal experience and what was passed onto me my father who I had spent most of my professional life with for as long as he was alive.

This book represent's a testimony of actual event's that transpired and are most likely the reason for my existence. I am a writer with a message for everyone
we must reverse the current trend of our society's
method's before it is to late.

We are all effected and that closing a eye is the worst possible thing that can be done or allowed at this time.
God is not going to help us if we don't help our selves.
We must have more than respect for one another there
must be a beneficial compassion in our lives like it or not because the forces of True Evil will prevail if we do not.

Jim Ochwatt

True Evil Never Dies

Table of Content's

Chapter

1.   Origin of Evil

2   Time Line of events

3.   Decline of a society based infrastructure

4.   Trade embargo's spin up and escalates

5.   A hypocrisy feeds the corruption

6.   Blind leaders don't want to see

7.   How the Phoenix fly's

8.   The suicide mission

9.   The transformation

10.   Deficit of knowledge

11.   When it comes down

12.   Who is going to pay

13.   The Responsibility

14.   Total abuse of power

15.   Two party's one agenda your money

16.   The effect

17.   Expectations crises

18.   Training system failure

19.   What can be done

20.   Under minded

21.   Deceitful Promises

ACKNOWLEDGMENTS

The Writing of this publication began at the beginning of the 2008 summer Olympics , and that the world's focus to that event was taken away not knowingly at the time to what is considered a financial world melt down of monetary system's , the irony is that it had taken place / began as soon as the Olympic games ended, and fully defined the severity in September of 2008. This problem has been in the development stage for the past 30 years. Because of such a problem going un-checked the severity is pronounced at this time as a milestone in the up-heave of society values as they have been known. This caused most societies to re-evaluate their goal's , and aspiration's of methodology in how daily existence is perceived . The financial wizards have all been exposed as dishonest and non sincere contributors to society , in as much the governmental institutions that should have provided over sight and limitations to circumvent such practice's were equally guilty in their neglect and duties to society. They work with out adhering to rules or fairness, and that they have caused the irresponsibility that has led to much suffering.

The outcome of their mindless greed effect's the poor , the helpless , the un-supported.
What if anything that has been learned by all this is what not to do , because the out-come result is a harsh lesson for those that are not multifaceted and or able to spring back from such condition's that have effected them.

For those that think that God is going to fix thing's good luck it's not going to happen. God does not support the teaching's of government officials to be or have any kind of reverence when you are talking about spiritualism. Remember it was government officials that condemned God .

It has now been proven that the result of a cultural / ethical breakdown in society values is being taught by the greedy and or corrupt, and that there methods have infected the world, and if not circumvented, the world will suffer until such a time that it decides the suffering and un-equality must stop, and that any repairing effects have to made based on acknowledging the root of where the problem grows from.

The failure of respect and or adherence to the life goals and understanding's of knowledge that is developed by experts that normally develop such knowledge after years of earnest work and understanding. The corrupt or ignorant people in control of the power and or financial institutions found it more desirable to ignore such important topic's , and that quick money was deemed as the order of the day in place of integrity.

There were plenty of people that had foreseen the event's that had taken place. They were ignored in that most people did not look at the reality of cause's and effect's that are part of such a disorder to society. If advocates of order are not installed it can only worsen the situation. There is no amount of money that can educate people to the reality of such thing's , and that only by a cultural awareness can we begin to un-do the damage that has gone on. The suffering and devastation comes from not foreseeing the so called unenviable. The unenviable could have been circumvented and it was not.

Chapter 1.   Origin of Evil

Most people think , true evil exists because of the lack of faith in
God. This notion could not be more wrong. The lack of faith in
God comes from the evil that would have man kind believe such a
thing. It is then further propounded by the people of the world that
would find it convenient that such things are perpetuated and further
elaborated on. For example if the leaders of the country's of the
world could not invoke fear and ignorance, in that nothing can be
done to stop the persistence of evil , except to combat evil with evil
,they would not hold there position of dominance. Or if they could
not escalate the effect of their supreme dominance, in that they the
few the chosen ones and only thru their system, are able to defeat
the evil, and protect the innocent.

This is truly animalistic as in the dominant male of the herd , he will
be the example of the leader of the herd , until of coarse he becomes
to old to hold his position , and then he is conquered by a younger
stud. This is the origin of a tyrant and how he demonstrates his
prowess. I guess it is very similar to wild animal behavior .

 This has always been the case, and that history holds records of this
to be true. The leaders of the great powers of the world for the most
part , have only had prosperity as their main agenda, and that they
have intimidated most people into buying into their propaganda.
More so in this day and age than ever. These leader's of the world
speak of evil as if it were humanly possible to be placed thru the
effect of evil taking hold of a persons soul and actually generating
some kind of dark force. This form of Ideology is persistent in free
world leader's and or dictator's both. The confusion comes from
the fact that free democracy's and or dictator ship' have behaved
similarly .

There is only one true evil and it is simply ignorance of the truth and the lack of it. We the human race are a society based group of mammals that instinctively want to believe and are compelled to believe in our superiors , as to give significant meaning to our existence. A compelling notion in that we must have strong and beautiful shinning examples of leaders , and that material gain, along with such beauty is the true meaning of God , and that we want to believe this because it is what , we dream of and what we were taught since children . So what's wrong with being successful, nothing however how you attain success is what the big question is.

People have and will continue to say its just the way of the world , only the strong survive, the big fish eat the small one's , and so on. In that this is true it is where much confusion comes from. So are we just a bunch of fish , wolves , bear's , and so on. I don't know about you but I am a human being, and the idea that someone would try to tell me I am just a animal so why bother worrying about it, is just about the most ignorant thing I have herd of. Have you ever herd of a animal that would not defend its nest or off spring, because I have not. In fact animals have behaved very inspiring when it came to defending their own. They seem to be guided by some kind of compassionate force that would be self sacrificing , if need be. There have been many occasion that animal's have done so for their human master's. It's also common knowledge that most animal's only kill to survive so that they would be able to continue to sustain.

Human animal's have been given a brain like no other animal, and that we have a through knowledge of all the animals, organisms, and physics that control this planet.

It would seem that we must be one of the oldest species of animals in that we were able to survive where great animal's with giant size brain's could not. Or maybe it was because of our size, and that it lends well to be adaptive. Now maybe you buy into the Adam and Eve theory I guess that's possible if you want to believe that a

Jewish person was the first Human species' personally I find that theory a little hard to swallow especially when there's mountain's of scientific data that show's this theory to be impossible. However what ever that origin was that had taken place to lead us, and perpetuate us, it must have been very difficult a long time ago, in that we had none of the things that make life easy now. That is except for one thing that is probably responsible for our existence to persist than and now, and that very important primal thought must have been love. Imagine that just a basic emotion being responsible for life, or a future of what life offer's . In one respect it may have been the deciding factor in weather one thing takes place or the other.

History has shown, and as well the present time that when there is a lack of understanding because of misfortunate occurrence's that had taken place. Weather man made or a act of nature , we want to explain it and attribute such phenomena as supernatural, witchcraft, lack of God, lack of discipline in serving god, and so on. To further explain this point , you could say God or Evil is the reason that un-educated people would commit to attributes and conditions that would cause horrific instances to take place , like people committing acts in the name of God or because of Evil and so on. If you look at a class of the elite and or fortunate group of people that control the destiny of the world you would than see that there goal in life as they were raised is to manipulate the un-educated, and or the un-empowered. In most case's such people or society's lacked understanding of the science's, art's, psychology, physics' , and so on.

This take's place, mostly out of a social acceptance standard that has been taught to them since they were young by there parent's peer's , and predecessors, and that they do not know any better in a lot of cases you could than say that the educated are actually ignorant of the truth, This effects all thing's that are connected to society in the daily routine of business and life and will eventually have a effect that transgresses to the less powerful and than , back to the perpetrator's them self's, History has shown that this is true and that the only way to reverse such a trend is to go against those that perpetuated such thing's, in the case of the United States , my country was saved from oppression by people that lived thru such a time period. These people that went against the corruption were the less fortunate , the oppressed, the poor, and yes the un-educated.

It was at that time recognized that it should be the duty of US citizen's to stand against the oppressor's , as to not be consumed by the Ideology of the corrupt suppressors.
However it has been more than two hundred years since these principles have been put in place and that there meaning's were distorted , confused, suppressed, and made to serve the purpose's of a growing system that because of it's size, and the corruption of other rulers , has lost a very important part of the meaning for which such principles were invoked. As time and progress in the material world of science has progressed, other societies that followed the brave meaning's of the U.S. have come up and that they too have regressed in their initial meaning's. This has all taken place for the sake of profit for the elite, and left the true workers of the U.S. and many other country's powerless to stop the corruption. Only a cultural revolution can change such thing's, that have come to pass. Peace , hope, and truth seem to be a thing of the past, in that this might seem to be true , there never was peace not since history had begun to be recorded, the corrupt one's made sure of this.

They all used the excuse that war was required because of a threat, in that this is true , it should be noted that being defensive, has nothing to do with being aggressive, and or the aggressor. In order for a cultural revolution to take place , wars must be waged on the basis of defense only, and that if a aggressor is to be put out of power it must be done with timing that would lend it self to a defensive nature. This gives meaning and a real reason to show that it is a matter of survival , and in most case's thru out history the

4

defining moment where true heroic value had taken place.

One such case would be that of the example by Jesus Christ. He selflessly demonstrated love and compassion at a time in history when it seemed that no such values existed that could be spiritually upheld. This inspired people and caused the failure of the current raining corrupt society in Rome. Rome was for the most part the dominant force in Europe / world at the time. This being the greatest example ever recorded when the power of reason stood against the power of corruption, and that the goal was to expose such corruption for what it was. Proper timing was involved the entire ordeal was contemplated and planned after all how could a God be hurt by mere mortals.

 The world was never the same after the occurrence, and that emulations from that point forward were demonstrated, and or inspired acts performed in the name of such nobility. The story of Christianity that is based on the King James New Testament is understandably not excepted by the predecessor story the Old Testament , for one simple reason it changed the rules , there was a modification , in how people developed a higharchy of philosophical belief's out of tradition , this did not sit well with people that worked hard at developing a corrupt system, that lent its belief's towards making a profit over people being honorable profits. Or that fear and intimidation was not as powerful as love and compassion. Instead it told of a current revelation that had taken place in the form of Humanism having precedence over myth's, and that transgressions were witnessed by people, the unification of thousands of people thinking of one soul that lived and breathed for there unity of gaining a practical knowledge that could be enjoyed by everyone including Jews or any other race of people.

The fact that King James had paid the scholars of that time to document the testimonies that were handed down is true and the fact

that there lives depended on it is also a little strange in that if they
did not document the testimonies correctly it would have ended up
costing the scholars their lives. This being the soul opinion of if it
was documented correctly by King James opinion a non-believer.
Very strange indeed, and it would lend a lot to the people of other
beliefs to wonder just what is the truth. How would anyone be able
to document such a history accurately to leave no question 400
years after the fact.

When Christianity had become a major power , it also became a
financial power as well , beginning with the first internationally
recognized example of how a International banking systems
operated , this was carried out by the knight's Templers's , one
reason that a lot of country's backed their system is it was formed
with being protective over it's depositors in the name of integrity.
This was a new and fresh Idea that went over well in that some of
the wealthiest institutions in the world that happened to like the Idea
of Christianity backed this system.. This was one of the origin's of
our current banking practices used today.

When Iraq invaded Kuwait , it should have been at that time , the
NATO powers dismantled the corrupt regime of Iraq. The Iraq
people would have welcomed such intervention, they were in fact
welcoming such a thing even after being bombed to Hell,
that's because they knew their leader was wrong, however when
you ignore proper timing you lose the one thing that is the deciding
factor in cultural change's , that being the people have to be with
the idea, and that their was distinctive measures of reform that had
taken place, and that those measures did not just drag a long like a
lame duck , and that for reasons they understood, with there limited
understanding. The current and past administration's of the world
have blundered their responsibility to them self's and the people
that they were suppose to be protecting. Or did they, because it sure
became very profitable for the elite, when these blunder's in
national and global security had taken place. One philosophy is that
it is the nature of war, as to why they profited, while this may be

6

true it was timing and a lack of a defensive front that allowed the offensiveness to take place. This is not a sufficient excuse for a society based on understanding the difference in such thing's , the so called educated , the protector's, and that they even considered them self's the reverent.

They have performed a very good job at perpetuating such thing's, from what I can see it could not have worked out better for them if it was planned, which leaves the question as to weather it was planned. How could people so educated be so stupid, by just that, it is not against the law to be stupid, for example if a person commits a murder and a court of law find's they were insane at the time they will not be sentenced to death in the U.S. or if they established that there was a constant lack of common knowledge that such a person was consistently demonstrating. If a person loses money out of ignorance they would not be held totally responsible. This process is manipulated by educated people, it is a game the elite have been playing for years and a cycle of event's that have caused the power's of rule , to organize and perpetuate such thing's to take place.

How ever what's most frightening is that , the world's destiny hinges on weather our leader's are corrupt or just plain stupid and un-attentive to the so called Evil that exists, by the way that was their educated description of the aggressor. This topic is related to economic, cultural, environmental, health and well being , and that I for one have experienced and seen the up-heaving of such thing's that have taken place in my, and my parent's life time.

As it was written , and documented by people that were intending to make common knowledge to all that would desire the knowledge, (in a religious fashion) , money, greed, and power would turn society's on each other, family's against their own, son's and daughter's against their parent's and so on, and that this has taken place in many case's, and in the widest aspect's it is taking place because of greed. Who ever coined the phrase , money is the root of all evil was not kidding. The fact is that such a thing applies to the rich or the poor.

These topic's are based on the informed having the knowledge that these thing's will come to pass just as sure as the sun rise's in the east and set's in the west. This knowledge is most valuable to survive as a society in today's world more than ever with the advent of man being able to travel any where in a few hours or obliterate our selves out of existence at the push of a button, not to mention the economic implication's that would be enhance and developed by those wishing to do so.

If the society's of the world do not concentrate their efforts militarily and socially on a defensive based plan we will surly be lost in that the powers that would evolve can and will take advantage of the un-prepared, and that they will do so with their version of substantiations in the form of religion, profit, and use for the most part their version that they have been suppressed. Let us not forget that the U.S. was brought down severely by a handful of fanatical mal-content's that believed they were doing this to further there cause and goal accomplishment (911) no doubt a shinning example of when the U.S. does not uphold a defensive diligence. Other example's pearl Harbor WWII, Europe WWII.

History has shown that after a war was fought on the basis, of a defensive nature and than after all was done , the winner's educated regulated, and monitored the aggressor country and aided to the rebuilding of it's infrastructures. This is how 20th century mercy and compassion would be recorded , this happened as the result of WWII.

Those country's were rebuilt prospered into super powers ,and that could easily destroy the U.S. and the rest of the world if they anted to do so today. However this will not likely occur. Those country's are very rich, because the U.S. buy's as much of those country's product that they can export. Money did not have a part in the U.S. and its allies in that the winner's and loser's all were disadvantaged as far as money at that time.

Money had no value , the entire monetary infrastructure was ran by the Heads of the acting Government agency's , and that all financial and or power status was controlled by Government , during the war.

What made the success of this Idea was simply peace and trust, and the idea of such a thing that was a common denomination that all society's wanted for their children , and family's. This process eventually demonstrated an ideal that showed and exposed corruption for what it was, simply by giving an example on how the correct and compassionate way was better for every one.

 It could be said ,and be very correct in doing so that the Ideal's of Jesus Christ were up held in the face of corruption , and that like it or not , humility overcame the aggressor, you could say that humility of the aggressor had taken form over confidence and caused them not to follow thru with the execution of their plan's properly. Is it possible that when Jesus Christ set such a example of humility , he had foreseen these things and knew them to be the standards that were to be played out thru history in the future, well I don't know but it sure worked out that way as history had documented, as if it was planned or for seen. One thing is for sure , the simplicity of such a Idea was sheer genius if it was planned .

According to raining government's , it was impossible for a carpenter , and a few fisherman by trade to have such vast knowledge. They were not the educated they did not attend the schools that the elite people did , how is it possible these people were so smart when the established criteria to have ordained knowledge came from excepted standard's that were considered the ruling powers of the world.   The only thing that has been proven is that people did not have a problem with killing there own for the sake of power and money. At least their consistent , that's what

9

they did to each other in the first testament also. It kind of makes you think what's wrong with these people, most races have the utmost respect for great philosophers that have been recognized.

When a race did sacrifice a virgin or perform another form of worship in what they believed to be for God's approval it was not done because a great voice came from heaven and spoke go and kill to make your self's worthy of my presence in your life or the whole village is going to suffer , not in my life time , how about yours , and if such a wrath of God did occurred 3,000 years ago it was not my fault , or any one else's since then. The world has recorded some real elaborate stories that would make the average person say what's wrong with these people.

Such Ideal's are no doubt extremely powerful, and yielded great result's , history recorded an event of triumph where hope seemed to be at a loss. It is very important to note that energy , and perseverance must be upheld by a goal, weather it be spiritual , the love of another , and or survival to sustain , these are thing's that have left the world inspired , given meaning to life , and or a reason to be faithful, and especially to show that the material world is only a partial aspect of life, and that the law of what seemed to be physics can be altered by the faithful, that's because if you don't have a physical advantage , and all you have to your arsenal is faith, a true scientific explanation of the translational effect's that have been recorded in history are substantiated by such practice's. OK this does not change physic's however its path has been altered , and the end result is manifested due to faith being the origin. Speaking of the material world , in that it should be defended it is only one aspect of a global picture in that after it has been fought over and stolen, and raped and pillaged and so on it is in need to be renewed as it has a limited life anyway, or a amount of resource's and in today's world in many case's it is exhausted of its defined capability and there for the main topic concerning the material world must be to conserve , repair, non-abusively exploit, and or to cultivate in a way that does not permanently destroy it's capability.

10

This is not on the agenda of the ruler's of the world, they do not respect, or value it, and that it is now apparent that there not going to change there methods unless it is forced onto them, if this be the ultimate case , there might not be anything left after they are thru, letting it go to hell.

History has documented that not until it was absolutely necessary , or a holocaust has taken place, or a great tragedy, and so on, that the institution's of the world acted to conserve or come to the aid, and for the most part it was too late at that point, because permanent irreversible damage had occurred. It is the same type of ignorance that, would kill a person that knew they were causing themselves to contract cancer from espouser to chemicals or radiation and so on, until it was to late, mainly because it did not effect them quickly and they could not see or feel the effect, however they were silently compromised , and despite knowing the out come they did not discontinue the affliction process, that could have saved their life. There are some people that in this fashion religiously think that God will take them , and restore them to grace irrespective to their sin's as long as they repent and ask forgiveness. If this is the case the great tyrants of history need merely ask forgiveness and all their transgressions are reversed. I personally would not have pity , what is truly frightening is that the tyrants of the world have no fear of God because they do not believe there is such a thing and that they do not want God to be , because this would not coincide with their corrupt plans.   Such idea's were probably installed onto them when they were children and that the effect multiplied as time went on.

 Children are very impressionable and that Ideas can be installed into them by the influence of freeing there spirit and giving them something at a early age that would be found amazing by them, and or so it would seem to be as they perceived sensation's , sight's , sound's , ect. that were new to them, and seemed to be the truth they desired, however if they were only shown a limited amount of example's , this would decide what they found to be truly the truth to them at that time. In using children to carry forth ideals it make's

11

the task at hand the fastest, possible route in accomplishing such goal's, weather it be for good or evil.

An important factor to consider , if there is a God it will , if it is just and fare, forgive the bad act's of a child because it would be known the child was influenced and not completely responsible for there action's. A tyrant reverts back to a child's mentality when it has been captured or stopped, and it will use for it's defense the most ridicules excuses to substantiate their action's, in hope for some strange miracle to take place that would save their worthless butt .

The people of the world need to wake up , and take a good look at what their financial and political leader's are not doing for them. They don't have there back , during the 1950's , 60's, & early 70's if you were part of the elite you did not have to serve in Korea / Viet Nam because you were considered a value to your country, you just had to be enrolled in collage , a notable collage and that got you saved. Thank god for the female nurse's that volunteered to serve. I guess there would not have been any drafted, another qualification that would have saved you.

My Father , his friend's , and most of the vocational training and support I received or supported came from military and or veterans of the U.S. Military , if it was not for them I most likely would not have gained the accomplishments I had achieved in my life. I had received Aircraft Technical & flight training from WWII , Korean , Vietnam, and first Gulf war active or veteran soldier's / officer's. from all the different branches of the military. These people saved my life, not from the field of battle , in that I was disqualified to in list because of a substantial injury I suffered from a car / motorcycle accident when I was a teenager, but because they influenced my life with purpose where the civilian government , and the elite , only tried to exploit me , and take what little I gained from working very hard for. When I was young I witnessed the same thing in that they did this to my father as well.

 Everybody needs to support there talk with some kind of appropriate walk that defines there view's. Some of the following examples should be considered, scientific data , physics demonstrations , battle scars from fighting to uphold the week , and or equivalent measures of time or sacrifice that caused you to arrive at facts that are of a benefit to civil right's , and or artistic creation, support and care for those that are to small or to week, or disadvantaged , and kept oppressed from achieving there God giving right to exist , like a human being. It would be honest in noticing that if you were listening to some one talk that had one of those backgrounds in the development of humanism they most likely have at least performed a noble act and not just talked one and in most case's be the best qualified person that would be suited for the particular relevant proposal that they would peruse. This is the normal scenario used to determine scientific data and or interrupt the qualification of a person's science / arts comprehension and knowledge status.

The point is that someone that is delivering a proposal on how they will achieve success , must base it on a working real-time scenario , projected outcomes are good but they have to be based on real time condition's . Real time solutions for real-time conditions are solved by people that have been experienced in a particular art form. In today's society our system structures have become complex so that they can serve more efficiently, however the art form has evolved and that experienced personnel must be available to engage the worlds operating systems correctly for uninterrupted service to take place failure is not a financial option that some burocrat is going to fix because he's the head bean counter dude. This is one of my main points in this book. It's also about the lack of education , compared with the requirement verses society population, draw. Let me put it this way , the population compared with the electricity example:

The population is a motor , the propulsion aspect of energy , The population is powered because of a battery , the battery is the earth. The power from the battery travels from the earth to the population via wires , the wires are boats , plane's , trucks , machines , factories , oil drilling , ect ,ect , ect. roads , everything else. If the batteries not big enough the motor does have enough power to perform well , if the wires are to small , they heat up and catch on fire , and everything burns up. However if the motor does not have a high enough rated peak output rating no matter how many , houses and trucks and planes & ect , ect , the population is not producing enough power , if the population related to society does not perform well , its because of being under powered , that's happened a lot of times , or it could suffer severe financial hard ship , that leads to all sorts of nasty things.

If this country does not explain real time policies in its federally mandated policy it is not exercising a conducive policy for the population requirements of the present time , this is unacceptable and poses a grave safety risk to the health and welfare of this country and that opposing views would be contrary for what the United States policy defines as its ultimate goal and or present requirements. I am sorry but the politicians that have been running this country don't have the first clue about what I am saying and that they have driven this country into the ground and burnt it up good. Being a politician is a pretty basic job to do , its like being a manager compared to actually having to comprehend or do the work required to accomplish things.

Now if you couple a little arrogance in with your , ignorance it makes for quite the concoction , and there you have it folks , some kind of joke you say , that's right the origin of true evil is a clown , just imagine all the ignorance and death and disease , poverty , etc . its all because of the joker, and you thought it was just a movie.

So do you really think that politicians are going to fix anything , who do you think supplied the material that the movie is based on. I was raised and grew up in the So-Cal., Hollywood , Santa Monica , Venice areas. They don't have that many talented writers that could come up with that many scripts , they had to come from somewhere. Just likes books , Barnes and Nobles , Amazon , ect. How could they employ all those authors , ect Government , real stories , bios , geographic , ect it all comes from the world , not Hollywood , they just know what to do with it, how to distribute it , publish it , exploit , ect. One thing you can be sure of is that if a politician is bad mouthing Hollywood or movie makers , there book is probably not selling well and they need to blame someone and the media has always been a thorn in the side to people that do not want to be completely transparent as a public figure head , there seems to be some kind of rumor that was generated in the United States that the people in California are nuts. All I can say is if were nuts around here how come were the ones that invent all the computers , space technology , medical break thru's, cultural awareness' , in all the arts , and science's , conservation pioneers , etc. yeah I guess we must be pretty nuts around here because a politician says so. Every one knows there the right hand of God. If they could just write some fair laws I am sure people would enforce them, I guess they should blame California for that too.

Chapter 2   Time Line of events.

Empires exist because there are workers at the bottom of the society chain that make up the supporting structure required. Lets take our western world system of society , and examine the process from beginning to maturity. I use the western example because it is the absolute system that has been refined in a industrialization that most of the world use's as a basic pattern.

The Empire system has been in place because society has put it there for many different reason's some of them good , some of them not so good , its been over 3000 years in the making. Most of the academic society based institution's are a collection of science art's that are both useful and needed.

A problem takes place when the financial leader's of that society become aggressively greedy and want to make more of a profit than is practical or fair. There focus becomes financially motivated. However this is not the origin or the development process required for proper development of the art's. Once industrialization of a society based art form take's place, the financial aspects take over, and true art or the world's need's are ignored for the most part, this intern cause's a deficit in capability to keep up with world demand / requirement and the inflation process begins. This Empire industrialization process also under mind's and belittles the true value and or concept's of their intension's. A substantial imbalance takes place , between class, & education capability, the sub-division's that take place next, create a lag and that as long as that lag continues, without being severely disturbed it will continue to compound based on population / inflation , and non-ability to achieve the base required to stop such a thing. To say the least a development of this process broken down to it's individual component's, is on a development level equal to the most complex

16

fact's of physic's . The topographical and natural aspect's in various world location's, are interrelated to make the process even more complex.

Young people are very intelligent today, mostly because of the advancement of science , and that analytical thought's are dominant in the youth's process of society analization. They will look at our leader's , understand the corruption for what it is, and plan or plot there strategies in life accordingly, this often times creates a deficit in true capability to the applied science / art's required today, and account's for the fact that there are far less qualified young engineer's and or technician's that are able to for fill the empire's required profit margin. This is not conducive for progressive initiatives to take place and only breed's contempt. This goes for just about every aspect of society, and that if this trend continues with out a cultural revolution the outcome will become even more, financially crucial. It is likely that severe and catastrophic economic failure will take place, at that point the inflation will become tremendous. We are already feeling the beginning effect's of this and if history demonstrates as it can not lie, it will worsen.

The empires will act accordingly as they are, and force the uneducated to take up arm's since it is such a profitable way to deal with this situation, and loss of life , property , hope's dream's will all be lost to death , disease , and destruction as history had recorded in the past. None of this is new but what's amazing , is that our society's are allowing it to take place in today's day and age. People have become submissive and have not just been allowed to think this way but that society has found such Ideals acceptable and much time / money is focused on perpetuating the Empire's goal's.

When I was about 5 years old , it was September in Southern California, and I was fortunate enough to be raised in an environment that was truly special, not because our family had money or prestige or anything real special like that but because it was an environment that was filled with all the normal natural aspects of the area that children could possible need for a good up-bringing, thanks to my father.

Well it was time to start public school life, and that even though I had never been to school, I realized at that time it was taking me away from the daily routine I was just beginning to understand and enjoy. I suppose if I was raised in a environment such as the one my father had been , as he related to me later in life, that being the South side of Chicago, IL. I might have welcomed school as a better alternative as how to spend the day. The early 1930's in the Chicago area was completely corrupt , the Chicago river was completely contaminated, this also was during the time of the great depression, and school was one of the only things a poor boy had to look forward to, for the most part as it was personally related to me.

So I started school, on the first day after we had lunch, I was told that I had to lye down along side all the other kids, for 1 hour , I was not tired and did not understand this I was than disciplined , and threatened with a bad report to my parent's if I did not due what they said. This was the beginning of my dislike for academic training, this continued for the most part all the way up to High School (not the lying down and taking a nap part). Thank god riddelin was not invented yet, I would have been ordered to take it by the school board for sure, although I doubt that my parent's would have gone for it. They did not have much money but they were very smart . The laws in the 1960's gave the school authorities permission to swat the kids on their behind with all the force a grown man could inflict. The reasons they performed such discipline's were ridicules, such as talking, or needing to go to the bathroom. When permission was denied you can imagine the philological effect to a young child , 6 years of age , that had taken place. They did not perform these discipline's on girl's . I told my mother what had happened at the first occurrence of such

discipline's, she could not believe it and she, went with me
to school the next day, to find out what the hell was going on, and
talked with the Vice Principle . He told her that I would have to
comply with any and all discipline's or be
expelled, from the first grade and there was not any other public
school's in the area. We discussed the matter and I did not want to
make a problem for my parent's so I submitted to the extreme abuse
practice that was the Los Angeles Unified School district
policy. You can only Imagine what was going thru my head , and
what I wished I could do to that son of a bitch. (I forgot his name).
 During the Vietnam war era, I did not ever here of a girl that was
drafted or made to be a infantry solider , this was understandable
mainly because of the absurdity at the time, of the condition's, that
young men were sent into, for conducting battle. Needless to say
faith in the system was destroyed by this time when I was around 10
years old . I can now appreciate that for a brief amount of
discomfort I endured how it showed me the true meaning of the
empires at a early age, and that although I hated these teacher's at
the time, and that they destroyed my academic chance's in my mind
I learned the truth in that their system was incapable to deal with
society correctly.

There were far worse effect's to our country's young men that had
taken place because of the mandatory draft. I did not suffer
anything compared with the less fortunate that were only a few
years older than me. I asked my father a few question's at that time
he being a WWII veteran.   Dad what is Viet Nam his answer to me
a avid supporter of the military, (ans.) I'am not sure, (ques) will I
have to go there (ans) I hope not. (ques) what is a Watergate (ans)
a swimming pool where grown men play game's with our
government. (ques) is that normal (ans) no.

He obviously was trying to explain thing's to me in a way I would
draw some kind of conclusion from. I could tell from the tone of his
voice and the look on his face that he was disappointed / disgusted

with our government. When I was older / able to understand the meaning's of his answer's I did not need further elaboration from him on those subject's. How ever he always reminded me that the system was cheating me out of a education.

 I could not have respected any one more for having true knowledge of what was happening in our society. My father had been to almost every place on this planet before I was born , and that he was highly respected by some of the richest and most influential people in the world. The best they could do for him was pay him $1,200. a month, for introducing a capability for such people to make million's of dollar's because of his technical experience in the Aircraft Industry, this was typical. And that he always put his family before his own pride, and that I witnessed on many occasion that, the elite would take advantage of him when ever they could. I thought that my father had the patience of god, and that nothing effected him nor was he humiliated by them he only laughed at their ignorance. I could not have had a better role model .

The point of my early child hood experience's is that society was threatened by the empire standard's and that you dare not question it's authority or suffer it's reprisal however the suffering would go on weather you cooperated or not.

Government Institution's / society's have and always will prey on the young, they are intimidated or persuaded easily and can be configured to take what was being propounded, and that for this reason it is important that the young people be motivated in a way that stop's the brain washing this is why the importance of a cultural revolution must take place. The young are the only hope for this planet.
They are open to the truth during the 1960's such a cultural revolution had taken place. It mostly came from the U.S. and England, and that because of it the world was changed. It was a great time to be young , and live thru an experience that made all

the difference in the world. Every aspect of life and society was effected. The applied art's and sciences, aerospace, music , film , everything was effected because of a want and desire for people to learn this stimulated economic growth, civil right's , and so on.

At the same time there was a bad effect, jealousy had set in because it changed some thing's . People that were not free spirited or part of the revolution felt threatened they mocked the change labeling it as bad or no good , or it would be better if there was a war instead so they could go back to the old way's and make a profit. They felt such a thing was a more correct path to take. They did not believe that what was happening was because of love and respect for other's and that such notion's were made up by young people that did not know any better. The truth is that they were the one's that did not know better because of the way the previous generation was brought up as a society, and or we were to young to make cultural change's. The world could not benefit from such a thing so they said. They could not have been more wrong or should I imply they did not want us to be right because in doing so they would have to concede they were wrong. A very strong and natural thought process is that no body wants to admit they were wrong it's embarrassing it might cost money, and so on.

In the case of religion the implication's are monumental, even if the mistake's that were made could be thousand's of year's old people are compelled by tradition. Who wants to say that there ancestor's were tyrant's or murder's and so on. Nobody however somebody was some society's were and history undisputedly document's it, and this is where Empire's draw some of there capability. It's a philological fact that people want to live together as a group , they are compelled to, this is human nature , for that matter all of nature and the physical world is held together by this fact.

Manipulative leader's and aggressors understand this, after all they are the educated , the fortunate one's, and they use this knowledge decisively. They sit on the side and above watch and study the factors that dismantle our city's , country's . Some may be saddened but will not step up and intervene. Some will laugh about it and blame their competitive peer's, as if it is a grand game, and it is to them because they don't feel the heart ache and pain, and so it is not real to them.

One of the manipulative trait's of the Empire system is to defend the traditional institution's , and that philology goes a long way in the art of brain washing.

Example: If your society is viewed by out sider's or other country's as a group that was responsible for atrocity's the leader's will make the innocent and guilty one's in that society seem to be a victim of oppression from a outside influence. This is what I call the Father figure. He will make false promise's, and accusation's while at the same time carrying out atrocity's. He is most likely responsible for thing's a 100 time's worse than , what he is accusing the foreign country of.

While there were member's of that country that were in fact responsible for such thing's the greater amount of the population was not however they will pay for the crime's of the few in many way's. When retaliation takes place the focus is directed to view the situation as a whole at this point everything has escalated and has become uncontrollable or irreversible. This is the snowball effect and a fact of physic's.
 In the coarse many innocent's are made victim's , this work's well for the tyrant's and was just what they needed to fuel the rhetoric to follow. Even if you cut off the head of such organization's the ignorance , and hatred will linger on far after the principle has been stopped that's because all they were ever taught is that they were a victim. When there country was blasted back to the stone

22

age it sure looked that way so you can see the after effect.
It lingers on as pain does after the hurt was inflicted, and the
following successors use it to drive the society system in ways that
rally it's subject's to participate for the idea's that the corrupt
leader's use.

The greatest and most horrific example as far as sheer numbers go
at any given day that would take place in the past 100 years that
sticks in my mind is the Atomic Bombing of Hiroshima / Nagasaki
Japan. Although the leaders of that country and the leader's
of Germany might have deserved such a thing strait up there ass,
there were hundred's of thousand's of poor men , woman, and
children that did not commit any atrocity's that their leader's were
responsible for nor did they have any desire's to, nor were they
military personnel.

 Like the German counter part they were ordered to submit or die.
Those that were the young and strong , and told that they were
being honorable to god and there country in Jesus name. Much like
the Moslem's that were ordered to comply by Sadam Husane or die.

Psychology was used to bring the rhetoric up to speed and it is the
only way it can be combated. We can only teach by example, and
that if our example is retribution , than that is what will be viewed
by the people. However if our retribution amounts to consideration
and or compassion that is what will be viewed after the fact.
Remember when Rome was brought down, it was because of (in
part) the sword of reason. It was not because of a single great army
with weapon's and specially trained soldier's. History record's that
the greatest battle's that ever had taken place were fought in
defense. Perusing such moral's that are exercised is unstoppable.
WWII is a great example as to the response by the U.S. / Japan and
Brittan / Germany. The power of reason goes very far when the
people are motivated, any people. Just as the people were
influenced to carry out harmful Ideal's they can be taught that peace
and trust is viable by showing a example. The most heroic examples

had taken place when the odds were stacked against the side of good and that they prevailed out of superior intellect.

So who's right and who's wrong well the answer at this point despite who started what is that ignorance and bias will not fix anything , and or pointing finger's does not work either. What matters is action. Who is willing to act on behalf of the needy, and innocent. Intelligence is the answer , and that's because ignorance and greed started the problem , and you must combat your enemy to a equally responsive degree. This will carry out a more forceful amount of energy in this case peace, and tolerance for a situation that is a lingering problem.

Authority held the few tyrant's responsible and made them pay but it will not bring back the innocent that are now gone. That innocent number compared to the tyrant's is a million to one. Were these few despicable tyrant's worth the life's of a million innocent. I think not. We acted responsibly to take care of some tyrant's but did we work as hard to protect the innocent. This is the question and no amount of politics' will help the pain that has taken place.

The leader's must be held accountable there is no doubt but how that accountability is perused is the key to the quest. It has to matter if thing's are to change with out innocent people suffering other wise it will be viewed hypocritically regardless as to who did what.

If history is a mirror to the trial's and tribulation's for society's causing change to take place than as a intelligent race (all human's) we must act on the basis of past action's. As much as science has upgraded it's capability. So must the moral value's that are used to define the process with dealing's pertaining to tyrant's in society. If we are not smarter or better than a tyrant than we are just as ignorant in a way that renders us under prepared to deal with the problem's at hand. No body said it would be easy many a good man and woman were cut down before their time that lived for such prepared value's. Let us not waste their compassion by being selfish or closing our eye's or turning away.

If society's do not show the correct response to ignorance they will be judged by what ever there response would be. During the Russian / Cuban missile crisis the rhetoric was to act as the aggressor was behaving. If this was carried out by President John F. Kennedy the whole world would have most likely been obliterated. Reverse psychology saved our country and possibly the world. Humility, and reason contained the situation and it was eventually demonstrated that the aggressor was wrong and that when every thing was said and done the ultimate humility was absorbed by the aggressor. That was a great example as to how to deal with ignorance. However by embarrassing the aggressor the peers of President Kennedy were also embarrassed because reason saved the day when aggression did not.

There were those that felt war was a better solution and President Kennedy paid the ultimate price for having the insight and knowledge to know better as did his brother Robert may God bless there soul's in eternity. I know I am alive today and the world is that much wiser because of their ability to do the right thing, and understand the extent of the corruption in their own system as well as the adversary's. Society need's such insight today if it is going to survive. The effect of cultural awareness, and the difference between having money, and being inspirational or greedy make's all the difference in motives that are exercised.

These rules don't pertain to the aggressor's because they can achieve their goal's irrespective as to where globally they attain their supply's to carry out their mission. How ever if there is a God they are going to hell for sure if anyone is. I personally don't take much stock in religion and repentance to me is a excuse for being ignorant.

To die for a noble cause should be valued as the greatest thing a human or animal could do for one another anyone that does not understand this is as ignorant as one can be. We should hold such hero's to a reverent status. If for only the reason that they believed in such value's, and that they are not made into martyr's with out a cause. History has taught that such effect's have transpired and were used by successors as such effect's. This is truly the greatest result of respect for the dead and injured that were true patriot's.

We live in age here in the U.S. / free world where such belief's are now acceptable criteria in the main stream media, how ever it is not yet been achieved in the real time world . The good news is things eventually take hold given a chance, and that the young people today can execute such initiative if they were so bold, and or up to it. Some of them are some don't care some are ignorant however like it or not all should participate. A factor that contributes to the facilitation of change is the time table as it relates to cutting down the amount of time to comprehend and possibly initiate new and creative acceptance .

Chapter 3   Decline of society based infrastructures

When society's are neglected it becomes everyone's problem to the extent of particular race's and culture's that were developed and brought to a development stage. Once the population of that region has exceeded it's capability to sustain even on the most basic stage of development it is breeding hazardous hidden effect's. The same way a lethal virus or pelage is activated, and spread just by natural condition's that would cause such a effect to take place.

This intern will effect the entire region , and force the compliance to tyrant's rule by the surviving people that are left. This cause's social behavior distortion's , and leave's nothing but turmoil in it's wake. In that there are relief society's that will feel sorry for such people after the fact including church's and ministry worker's a lot of time's it is way to late to combat the out of control effect's.

In most case's the local regime's have taken over the situation's making it impossible to salvage the effect properly. In as much as this breed's the social, and local capability's of a region powerless the cost's to other society's that can help is very costly due to the civil war and or regional conflict's that would take place.

This could have for the most part been avoided in most case's if the people that came to the aid would have come to the aid before it got out of hand. Such organization's that call them selves humanitarian aid and relief organization's and or military organizations are excepting responsibility for things it would be cheaper and easier to get it right from the beginning.

Not a easy task however the world has no choice if it wants to be left with anything after the fact. There are so many man made disaster's and than you have the natural disaster's, and than everyone's system becomes over burdened. This is what the tyrant feed's on this is when he sits on the side laughing at the helpless situation spreading his wings like a vulture ready to pick apart the dead pray watching it deteriate, so they can plot there strategy.

I have herd lot's of people debate what started what or what happened or this or that but people seem to be reluctant to want to admit that it is comprehensible as to what happened, and that they should have acted decisively, and that in the future they wont let it happen again. Yes they always say these thing's and they mean it at the time but they don't stick to it, and the same neglect for a situation is repeated time and time again. This leads to the probability that it wont change and there will be another repeat.

The tyrant knows this he's counting on it in fact he's using that very knowledge to perpetuate his propaganda and to turn the whole thing around and say that it's actually the humanitarian's fault. So there is much responsibility for a society and or aid contribution center to stay the coarse the alternative is failure, and far more costly for everyone.

When I say everyone I am referring to the entire human race, and were not talking about some day it is in fact happening now and has been for year's. At this point the beginning of August 2011with the U.S in a multi trillion dollar deficit it could not be more clear as to what is going on and who was responsible for it at the beginning and present time. Any time there is a condition that would promote imbalance of a democratic society there is a global effect to society's population. This is a condition that will promote all the wrong thing's to take place and the innocent to suffer the most unjustly effects that any one would. All because of the worst reason's imaginable greed, pride, offensive disorders, and so on. It beguine's regionally but thru evacuation or refuge population's it is made global very quick. All the planet's, food and energy , and for that matter element's , mineral's , are linked together to accommodate the growing population's and expanding regional growth's . If a setback in growth standard's are present it is very difficult / or impossible a lot of the time's to every repair or replenish a capability.

There must be accountability programs that are maintained from a budget that promotes region maintenance of a society system. This system must be maintained by the region, and or the supporting society's that are responsible for commerce taking place from such a reason.   You could call it a tax that if not paid will cause suffering to everyone.

In the past tax's have been looked at like some kind of necessary evil how ever the system work's when the main contributors are the entities that are gaining or earning the most. The problem occurs when the poorest and most needy are taxed the most , and are up holding the leader's of a empire. This plane and simple is not just greed but True Evil in that there is a system of law's that will punish the young the week and needy if non compliance to such a corrupt system is not complied with.

This is the true root of the problem , and that in many case's what little material thing's such a poor society is in need of will be deigned. Their own leader's in pursuit of personnel gain will proclaimed for them selves that the poor will comply and if not die from lack of a basic requirement to sustain. It is not difficult to understand this just ask the people that are effected and they will make it very understandable to anyone. Now this effect's the greedy even if they don't realize it or maybe they do realize but just don't care because they just want to make a quick buck. Or get a cheap thrill or play the system like a game get what they can when they can get it.

NATO / World society's are suppose to understand this, and that

29

nothing will grow if basic human right's and need's are
not met , and maintained. There must be a universal monitoring of
Humanity need's being continually maintained . If this is done than
every thing else that should or could be accomplished will have the
correct basis to be planned and set into operation. That includes
military action's that might be required for a more severe
or corruption dismantling process.

The people of a effected region must get behind a necessary action
or the after and during result's will not develop the desired
outcome.

The true key to success besides cooperation in such thing's is the
integrity of those operation's taking place. As well as integrity the
mindfulness of a distilled plan of operation should be developed to
form the regard for such practice's. This should not be
accomplished after a aggression has taken place. That's because the
situation has gotten out of control. Aggression must be stopped in
it's track's , and or simultaneously. The wait and see scenario doe's
not work and under mind's the integrity of maintaining a ongoing
un-stable area and or social condition. Thing's don't just happen
overnight in respect to a society up-heaval it is not like a terrorist
act or suicide bombing unless you want to include the fact that
planned , plotted , and or event's that had danger signal's were
being ignored or disregarded out of ignorance. Collapse of a
society start's at a demoralizing level , and that when whole
society's decide to do the wrong thing that's when it occure's. Let's
make some comparison's of event's that will elaborate on this
general Idea of how it work's regardless of the society ethnic , and
or wealth status.

Example: 1

The general consensus's of its people in relation to the ruling party
control is money survival , economically , spiritually , if thing's

look like it will work for them they go with it. They often time's find out later that their leader's were not acting on there behalf or with their best interest in mind and that they might have been misguided, and made to do the wrong thing out of ignorance and or the wrong decision. The bottom line is that the leader of such corruption is at fault, and must be held accountable.

Now if we kill the corrupt leader of a society this only emboldens the society and makes the corrupt one a martyr and further inflames the situation, and worsens it bedside's if he only ordered atrocity's to be carried out and someone else actually committed the physical crime you must in all fairness hold the actual perpetrators to the same responsibility even if the leader is the devil himself. Besides if you are killing someone in the name of God, it was God that sent the Devil here to earth to teach us all not to screw around.

Conspiring to commit a murder is different than actually carrying out the action. That mean's the soldier's that did the raping and pillaging should be condemned in the same way they condemned or killed or murdered. These are the laws of western civilization and they must apply to anyone and everyone.

It has been said and reflected upon that sometimes with certain individual's that being a captive and reduced to nothing when you use to be king is sometimes worst than death it-self for many reason's . It is also a fact that if you imprison a tyrant and use him as a embarrassing example to him self and other's that you are showing the rest of the world that such a tyrant was just a human being and that if he was religiously rightful how come he became captured or why does he not take his own life the way he manipulated other's to do so.

These questions will be raised in the minds of the less educated and there for making them educated on what not to do or how it is not a good idea to be part of a failed network of hostility. Things are not

31

what they seem and can become severely twisted and distorted. There is no excuse in this day and age for society's to act irresponsibly when a example of the result is made public.

This is the hope and inspiration for the poor , the shinning example that was promised to a small child's dream's , and that those dream's of such children , hold society's future hope and that proper guidance must be maintained to promote there development.

Their will be no more development's to maintain , and every body will be out of a job because there are no more worker's. Or they will have nothing to eat , or any soldiers or anything else that are required products that the young and strong produce for the world's population. So if society really wanted to solve this problem they would make this the priority of their objective. There is no shortage of young people that would volunteer for such a thing to take place if only the elders would show them how , they would ask only for the opportunity because it would be their future that they were pursuing. I know a lot on this subject I have personally been helped in life this way , and that I have helped other's in a similar way, and I can say undisputedly that it work's or doesn't work depending on if people participate.

The fact is that such program's were installed into the United States and Europe, how ever a lot of them have been discontinued. The reason used was money or no availability to fund such programs. Of coarse these are false reason's there is money for the procedure and it does not cost much. These program's must be maintained for society to keep up with it self or the indebtedness will cause a catastrophic effect felt through the word that is only compared with the devastation that war's would produce so if that's not a national security issue I don't know what is.

 The corrupt leader's of the world only understand what they are caught up with. They cannot make appropriation's for programs that they are not knowledgeable on or if there focus is on personnel

32

gain forget it's not going to happen unless a maintaining institution with knowledge is overseeing thing's constantly. If the senate of a country has become corrupt which almost all of them are than there must be a system to defuse that effect immediately. If we wait 2 or 4 or 6 year's before that corrupt power is voted out of power than it has become to late in the game. The true authority of judgment must lie with the people primarily the people that are doing the actual job of policing.

What good is having a United Nations organization if it powerless to have control of a situation when they were suppose to do such a thing in the first place. The worlds stage is truly global , and that a global entity must be the ultimate deciding factor in that it is there special job that they are to do that the world recognizes.

There must also be a agency that is in charge of the U.N. , and that the only logical choice for that agency must be given to the university's of the world , and that the ultimate responsibility would lie with the young people that are doing all the work in the first place and that they are also the losers if thing don't work out correctly.

If it is collage student's under the guidance of professors that are supervising the inventing and developing the newest technologies , and or demonstrating peacefully for the proper civil and human right's in any country yet our elder's don't recognize there authority even though they are the true expert's, the true future, and the ones that have paid the bulk of the ultimate sacrifice for ideals that are made and based on integrity , truth , and substantiations that have led to the development of the worlds society's, than it should be their duty and job to enforce integrity.

The particular student's that should qualify for such a position need to be of the technical expertise that lends to such a enforcement procedure based on the standard's that are non prejudicial such as the disqualification of marketing and or legal expert's, because those subject's are considered after the fact of what is the true origin of science or art which needs to be the primary reason for what is recognized by the world as non bias motivated, and the real requirement's of the world needs.

If this was not true than why do the corporations of the United States depend on the development of the fabrication process / research in medical , Aerospace , all the science's , culture , art ect.. It's really simple our children are the reason we have anything , and or that anything will develop good or bad. If the elder's show an example that's bad than that's what the student will produce, if there is a example of good than that's what will be produced.

However to say one thing and do another and use the excuse that things change is not going to cut it. This only breeds corruption and contempt. There must be consistency in a legitimate procedure that is not circumvented for any reason. This was the U.S. policy established and exercised at the end of WWII.

Now the world has invested a lot of time and money for police dept. fire dept., EPA, FAA , IRS, United Nation's, ect. The fact that the world is becoming globally interdependent on each others region's financial recourse's / environment make's thing's complex and that a standardization of fair trade / market rules must be enforced by the expert's in their field , and overseen by regulation enforcement of those rule's based on a individual occurrence, and that putting up sanction's short of a full out confrontation does not cut it.

 Only the innocent will suffer, the rich will not have a problem because of sanction's that are put on a country. It will only cause strife and hardship for the greater of the population's , these are tactic's that the rich use to negotiate with the rich or power's of the sanctioned country. There is always going to be the effect of a middle man that will make it possible for anyone to get anything they want if this was not true than how come the drug trades are not stopped. the U.S. govt. knows where it comes from, they are a small number of outlaws compared to world power's.

We spend billion's of dollars on the war machine , so why is money not directed at the root of the problem, specific Intel. would be a much wiser and specific direction on what and where the problems are. They could be controlled before escalation had a chance to take place. It is no different today if a tyrant's plans are allowed to be taken lightly we will falter. How many more time's does the world need to learn these harsh lesson's.

 It should be the U.S. policy and of all nation's that want to insure the integrity of their awareness as to where and what the adversary is, and what they are doing , and how close they are, and so on. But that's only the first stage of a protection program, and a matrix of further solution's must be constantly upheld and maintained as to not allow thing's to get out of hand. That includes a dialog with real intention's and meanings that do not include retaliations that dissolve because of a group of fanatic's that don't represent the view's of the innocent. How much could it possibly cost to pay the policing personnel a fair amount for risking and giving there lives so that society can have their safety . To not do this instigates the basis for further aggression, and that when innocent men , women and children are killed the focus is not why it's who did this.

Hate trends are bread by ignorance due to a lack of understanding the circumstance's . My teacher's always told me 2 wrongs don't make a right. So if that's what they teach in public school's and we don't exercise this policy than it's meaningless, we are meaningless, what were taught is meaningless.

Apparently there is no country that ultimately teaches this nor is their a specific culture that does thru their policy's . There for we as the human race must except responsibility for acting like human beings with each other. Yes that's right human sanity is the answer , reason , humility , trust , peace , conservation, must be exercised always. It must be practiced and improved on and perfected and that includes with such duties a responsibility for up holding those duties.

Awareness of a aggressor and not underestimating the ability of a sick mind is one of those most important duties. That's what a police dept. is suppose to do at the urban and private sector level. This deployment of defense must be carried forth at a national level with out rendering a misleading effect while doing so.

Such department's must be integrated within the community that they serve this is their primary duty it is always easier to negotiate a resolve than have to take on the aggressor at their level which often is necessary because thing's get out of hand.

The larger the event the greater the chance that thing's will get out of hand due to the amount of escalation that takes place when individual factions are transpiring that's why it is so important to monitor and maintain so as it does not get to that point. The problem is that government's that know the difference openly monitor and do not maintain. This is the main hypercritical problem.

If immediate intervention takes place, that is what could be considered truly divine as far as how to define such a series of event transgressions. If there is a bomb ready to blow and there is a bomb specialist there to defuse it, he gets one chance to do so. If he's good nobody dies , if he's not well it was noble that he tried but it goes off anyway .

If a virus out break occurs doctors have one chance to contain it, if they don't the virus escalates , and becomes a big problem. These are comparisons to social behavior pattern's . There really is not any thing different in how perception's and or real time attributes of circumstance's or procedures are played out. The greatest of the

Greek philosophers Aristotle had figured this out and thru his teaching's that the world recognized to be valid in 350 BC. He had taught and educated the leaders of that time of such things. These teachings are excepted and the basis for science , culture , medical , and most of the currently excepted world standard's of today.

A prerequisite for educating social behavior is being a teacher, in that all teacher's must have knowledge of psychology, related to the learning process , so that proper steps can be taken to enhance and usefully teach , this includes why a person or animal would be aggressive , or why they would not engage in the process properly , or why they are embarrassed, and so on. If our diplomatic dialog does not have people that are versed in understanding human nature nothing can be done properly . This does not apply to the individual that has no intention of conducting anything properly.
This is known as a hostile participant and or factor. If the un-willing participant try's to use your theory against you , there are not many option's at this point. If the participant is the ruler of a country and is trying to make his subject's behave improperly the last resort of the teacher is to humiliate him. You must not be fooled by his aggression in that it frightens you to stand up to him , you must also show that the joke is on him. This will show the people he intimidated that he is not a God or the tyrant they need to fear but merely a sick individual that is really powerless when he has said and done every thing that he could.

This will be the successful plan that can be repeated on a continues basis. You can't argue with a sick mind so the first thing to do is identify the sickness , the multi national preferred and successful procedure of choice in explaining to a society that is fearful of corruption is to, demonstrate , explain , discuss , and review. This way the entire process of a topic is thoroughly gone thru , and gives the people a basis for your procedure and as to what should be expected from them , so that a better understanding is brought forward as to illuminate any miss conception's or explanation's to such process's.

If you just tell some one this is what the deal is and that's it without any explanation as to why you are saying a certain thing they will resent it , or not except it , and give them selves a reason why they will not listen to you, despite if you are telling them the truth or not.

This is a basic human trait that is a acceptable explanation in all cultures and society's, and what separates reason from a tyrant. There must be a coalition that will insure the safety of cooperating local people. People that have cooperated in causing the aggressor to be brought down must be relocated for their protection sometimes so that retaliation by the aggressor or any of their agents cannot take place, this will help to eliminate fear and cause a trend to take place until the aggressor becomes the aggressed of their own making, this to will cause imbaresment of the aggressor, as long as the poor people continue to turn on the aggressor in numbers they will not fear this solution. However I must stress that to accomplish it is sometimes required to relocate the innocent, there is sometimes no other acceptable way to do this. Any society regardless of their ethnic back ground must be comfortable in this procedure because there are always going to be corrupt people trying to angle a profit for their cause. All possible options of the aggressor must be eliminated. This procedure is actually 1000 times more economical than if the situation becomes full blown or aggressors fully take over.

We do this in the United States under the witness protection plan when dealing with organized crime, the alternative is living in fear.

Patience and reason must be contemplated , and that most society's are compassionately based in their ideology. Responding to a tyrant's demand's must be a well thought and planned response taken into consideration, this is difficult because there is always emotionalism that is infused with a situation that has gotten out of control.

38

One way to stop organized corruption is to turn it on itself sort of to speak such as to make it look like a rival faction was responsible for the intel that led to bringing down the corruption. There is really not a nice way to deal with such situations except that you must be more clever than the aggressor and take into consideration all aspects that would insure that the innocent are safe. If you are dealing with a snake you must be more wise than the serpent that crawls on its belly.

If a society's infrastructure has been compromised it is a major project to deal with such a situation. History has shown us that when you ignore the warning sign's it only leads to further escalation and or further deteriation of the situation. Things will not get better by hoping when corruption has settled in, it is a cancer, a laceration, a broken bone and it must be attended to by professionals that are earnestly pursuing their craft with total knowledge of the situation. There are not enough bomb's that can put down a infrastructure that is living in corruption. There is only one real answer and that is to stand up to the aggressor in the same way you would be aggressed. Do onto them as they do onto you, out smart them at their own game.

This is the noble and effective way to deal with such a situation and that you will win the heart's and the soul's of the people. History had shown that after a man named Jesus Christ inspired the people , and was tortured by the hands of the so called powerful all they did was expose them selves for the true cowards they were. Think about it how is it possible that one man with no army , could be a threat to the Jewish and the Roman Empires, because he was a man that spoke of fairness and peace.

All I can think of is that, he must have truly performed some miracles or transgressed as his apostle's claimed or that he and his key apostles James, John, and Peter common fisherman were so intelligent that they were able to convince all the good people in the world of a grand hoax. If that was the case they must have been the smartest adversary's to corruption ever known. What ever the case his nobility inspired the world to bring down the Roman Empire and that the world was forever changed after he came and went.

From then and up to now people have been so inspired that they were willing to die for his cause I think mostly because his cause was just and he bled and died so that the innocent might not have to. He had faith in God and his faith was not in vain because the people took up his cause. Now that is true power weather you believe he was the son of God or not.

Obviously there is no better way to demonstrate a cause than to show a example. After an example is brought forward it was explained as to why this is one thing over another and how the two different topic's are related. The topic's are than discussed among anyone interested in such concern's, and that after such knowledge is completely understood to the fullest extent possible a review of all thing's will have transpired.

Such things can be analyzed and reviewed by everyone at this point this would put a aggressor at a disadvantage if his rebuttal was not sensibly based. The aggressor's rebuttal no matter what it could be would not appear to have validity due to the fact that it is based on aggression, and aggression is not part of the normal human desire it is antagonistic in nature and that women , children , the elderly , and other's that have their emotion's based on compassion can not except aggression not to mention that a aggressor him or her self does not desire to live with aggression all the time.

They must rest in peace or go insane they must eat what is a product of man or die from only eating or drinking what comes from the earth that is not man made. Roman soldier's gained strength from wheat, and enjoyed wine. Human civilized life is society based , and that it must be perpetuated by wise values. The Garden of Eden just doesn't cut it folk's.

Chapter 4   Trade embargos spin up and escalate corruption

When a trade embargo is mandated against a country with a corrupt
leader this only causes the innocent to feel the pain of such a thing.
At the same time it feeds the rhetoric of its corrupt leader. As the
embargo furthers its strife put on the masses, it furthers the corrupt
leaders hold on its own people by forcing them to comply with his
wish's of totalitarian based society. The people are forced into
compliance out of necessity , hard ship, and further ethnic cleansing
is propagated. The week and oppressed parish , and the strong and
aggressive prevail.

At this point many forms of fanaticism can progress, for many
different reasons, and the problem reaches a escalation point that
cannot be reversed as fast as it had taken place. This further
complicates thing's , and leads to many different forms of idealism.

The business of sanctions make's it appear that the one's putting
forth the sanctions are suffering some kind of financial difficulty .
Just the opposite is what's really transpiring. Such is the case with
to use the best example oil. If a middle eastern and or south
American oil producer is sanctioned this drives the cost of oil every
where up in price because it is a commodity, and the price of a
commodity is dependent on the qty. of available product if less is
available it is worth more. The sanctioned country will sell their
product to a different country at a higher price , and than both
country's make more profit .

 If that's not the case than why is Exxon / Mobil able to make
historical profits when there is a so-called shortage of oil , and or if
the cost per barrel drop's they just sell more oil. There is a reason
for everything things don't just happen , the stock market does not
just go up and down because someone is having a whim and

decided that it's a trend or some other B.S., and that the people that buy into such rhetoric are kidding them selves or some one else.

Modern day stock market values are technologically analyzed / driven with a global consideration, and that market's in foreign country's are commonly linked with each other although they have independent exchanges, the fact is because of the population of the world and the evolution of business and trade their markets are inevitable linked to one another, while retaining their independence.

There are strategic aggressive marketing / influence's that will work the crowd as I refer to the constantly altering changes in global economic and culturally strategic influences that take place , and are driving market trend's.

Other controlling factors for the publicly owned market's , that really need to be called privately owned because they are not operated by the government , and only regulated to a point , which makes their out comes manipulate able by global factors such as who's is at war with who , who's winning and who's loosing , its all just a game that is played by the powerful and the rich and or the broker's. The world is literally a off shore world that is governed by the Chinese because they have all the money.

This is a separate world from the people that do the actual work and labor that turn's out a physical product. It's always been this way and it always will be. It's like the weather a constant battle with it's self in the forces of equilibrium, that cause a effect due to a uncontrollable force, except it's man made, and carefully orchestrated by the element's of financial power. Do not believe otherwise or else you have deceived yourself.

Creating sanction's for any reason for any country is just plain a bad Idea , even if they deserve it. Once you have made the working class people of any country to feel disadvantaged because of a

country's policy's , this makes the sanctioned country's
people bitter toward that country, and in their eye's , no better than
their totalitarian ruler not to mention the rulers of the sanctioned
country spin it to a total advantage on their financial part. All that
the average person knows is they keep getting stepped on when
their trying to go forward. It is difficult to get ahead in those type of
countries and that everyone works hard for very little in return.

 Once the flow of material they have invested , sometimes
their hole life's saving's is gone, all hope is destroyed for a better
future this breed's corruption in that country to gain alternative
product's from alternative source's.

Some of the country's that the U.S. sanctioned , will and are going
to play a game with the U.S. and turn the sanction game around , in
the form of oil , mineral's , fruit's , fish , and or other global
commodity's. Once a country's particular stock market understands
the U.S. vulnerability pertaining to global commodity's, and
supplies these country's will buy up such materials and hold the
U.S. financially hostage , this coupled by the growing outstanding
debt that these foreign country's are holding , treasury bond's,
world bank note's, ect. they will be playing the game in reverse on
us , after all who taught them this game, we did and now every body
knows how to play the game.

Various world bank organizations are responsible for much of the
continues corruption that takes place and continues to exploit poor
income country's. That is there are poor income people that are
doing the labor of making it possible for the few rich corrupt leaders
to capitalize with the help of world banks that are funding ,
speculating , creating hedge fund based instrument's, and a
multitude of other non-benefit's to the people that are the victims of
smart, educated and dishonest leaders of such country's, and or that
they are backed by such. This is how a dictator is able to hold on to
his dishonest money that he has extorted by threat of militarism to
any who would expose him. It is also how a lot of people that work

for such banks are contributing to the upheaval that is taking place for the most part these bank employees are not aware of what they are contributing to and or the ill effects that are caused onto the poorest people in the world.

That's because they live in a whole other culture that traditionally has not known of such secrets that the main players are creating. However if you were on the loosing end of the game it might be a whole lot more clear as to what is going on and who is doing it. It would be fair to say there are innocent people on both sides of the spectrum. It is easy to see if you follow the trail of ignorance it will almost always lead to the innocent suffering the greatest amount.

The next people to feel it are the country's investors that have put on the sanction's. This in turn creates un-stable global economic problem's in many different area's. The world's stock market organizations stop investing in such product's based on research that would slow growth for any particular area . The only ones that benefit from this scenario are the largest company's. They have lots of money to play with. They have been playing this game a while, and they know from past records that all companies in all geographic location's are constantly moving due to the fact of once a certain product is developed in a certain area that local managers of that area have found cheaper out sources to get certain things produced in the less advanced area's of the world and they seek out these new and cheaper resources of production.

However this is expensive and only develops into a monopolistic type of arrangement and that only the strongest corporation's that are the smartest that have foreseen such events and have the resources will be able to compete in such market trading.

 It develops , under developed rejoins , and that this goes on naturally because of rising costs and values for any particular area's of development. Once a population realizes it's self worth compared to what they are receiving they will abandon there original work and or country if it is not to their expectation's. Almost every culture has been exposed to the world via the internet.

Development by the new producer is not ready to produce or other variable logistical developments are not in place or developed yet. This is jumping the gun and trying to force a economic situation without proper development , and is defiantly not a smart way to go. This is only the technical reason why such practice is a bad idea. If the shift is in a region adjacent and neighboring the previous producer there is a bad taste in the mouth of the loosing / previous producer , and that war's can be generated by such things taking place.

Lets say a major country that develops and sells arms, somebody's making a lot of fast money because of civil unrest simultaneously leading to stock market blunders onto un-suspecting investors. Wow I must have a vivid imagination some might say however I have personally wittiness such thing's go on. In the U.S. and other country's on various level's.

Think about this if you went to school to study and receive a degree in money marketing or the equiv. and this happened to the company you worked for, and you were in a top management position, and you were fired because somebody is always to blame usually someone innocent with out knowledge of such things. This would make you bitter and if that was your life , that just got flushed down the toilet you might start thinking of ways to not let that happen again and or how to get back at someone that caused such thing's.

This is a normal human response and that most people would take such a attitude. I personally was not raised this way so I have nothing to prove I can thank god that I had a very enjoyable life when I was younger, and did almost all the things I could have dreamed or planned at the time. My father always reassured me that

if you keep faith in your self, and go the coarse you will prevail
regardless of your set backs, and that a positive attitude is the only
thing that separates us from the tyrants. I once asked him if it was
not futile to engage in working with such people, and that what
purpose is there in such things if the outcome is known to not work
for me, or that I would be cheated without a doubt. His answer was
profound and probably the wisest thing anyone ever said to me. He
said if you loose faith in what you love , evil will inherit the earth
and you will be left with nothing.

He would know such things he traveled the world before I was
born, and that he earned quite a reputation for him self in being
great at what he did in life , and that every one that new him ,
admired , and loved him because of his ideals, and wisdom.

It was clear to me at that point ,what he was taking about, it was not
what you do in life its how and why you do it that separates you
from the average disbeliever. His life was based on faith and faith
did not let him down, not like most people, they are faithless
because they had no reason to have it, but if you
were raised on the south side of Chicago back in the late 1920's and
you did not know where your next meal would come from because
your mother left your father you had nothing except faith to go on
this either makes you strong or you give up, he never gave up, or
gave into corruption, or stole, or lied and always put his sons and
daughters before him self, and that he never deterred , from that
way of life ever.

For people that speak English and have a knowledge of what can be
done in this world it makes a solution a lot easier, for people that do
not have that basic trait, that many of us in the United States have
taken for granted it is almost impossible to break that cycle of
poverty unless you are extremely intelligent and purposefully
driven. This is something that you cant understand from watching
television and that you must take into consideration , because
believe me there are people that would give anything to have the

opportunity that so many of us feel is there birth right just because they were born here.

I was such a person when I was younger and thought such things. I did not find out how mistaken I was until later on in life when I did not have the simple things that were cheap and readily available 35 years ago. To all the young people that may read this book one day don't make that mistake, things don't get easier they get tougher as time goes on. This is taking place because society did not take into consideration the amount of time and money spent by people that do have it easier the elite spent plenty of money on false hype, peer pressure, and just plain making thing's look better than they really were. So when enough people buy into it, there goes the neighborhood, straight down .

Embargoes are relative to the neighborhood , they are going on and they are instigated domestically everyday, though you might not realize it, and it has divided this country between the different class of people. Something this country has had forced upon them by the leaders, and top money managers of the major corporation's.

Due to the lack of engineer's in design , production , and purposeful future development consideration's , the mentality of today has shifted from what is the best Idea , to what is the cheapest , and most profitable. This is decided by a class of people that do not have a clue of their own reality, that is destined to failure because of such arrogance.

How could you instruct , or inspect , or carry out procedures if you don't have any knowledge of such thing's . Only by someone having the insight to take the time to gain such knowledge can it be attained. I learned when I was young that you might not like or agree with certain person's habits or view points but if they produce what you need , and your not going to attain it from a other source you would be wise to learn what you could from such people to at least what would be considered the basic fair minimum

47

required by such, instead of trying to pick and choose the recourses you think you need from them, and shunning the other parts of solutions that they had the insight to proceed with.

In most cases such people don't have anything else in life planned and that what little they did, they have most likely perfected such things and are, conducting them at the cheapest and most economical possible amount that anyone could realistically operate at, or they possibly became very resourceful at gaining a foothold.

So the next time you think you don't need someone because you don't like their ethnicity , or their country origin , put yourself in their position, would you like to do what they have to for a living . Most managers would not I don't know of any in the U.S. and the next time you think that these people you depend on are a bunch of turnip farmer's , think about this ,what do you know about turnip farming, or how to hire a bunch of turnip pickers, or what is required to take care of those turnips so they don't spoil , or get contaminated. When a person has been a turnip farmer there hole life, and they come from a long line of turnip farmers they are, turnip professors, as far as your concerned, and lets not forget that computer scientists need to eat turnips to make you millions of high tech dollars.

I hope you understand that the example of turnips is to show the relevance on interdependence between the classes of people, and not if you like turnips or not, I have personally never ate a turnip that I know of , but from what I have herd there are lots of people out there that have , and consider them part of a ethnicity and culture that they are quite proud of . So if it makes you money because everybody else likes turnips, and it doesn't hurt anything why should you care, in fact throw them a turnip party, because you will be laughing all the way to the bank singing I love turnips.

The primary work force in any country cannot do anything with out the basic requirements of life , land is abundant. Food , clothing, gas , these things are not and they cost the same any where on this planet now because they are world distributed commodity's. The world market's are integrated to reflect a certain price based on , the exportation of any given region to participate in there country of origin and or trade market's and are set up based on the combination of those figures. The particular country's price is set on that basis and that it does not take into consideration any other variables such as the local needs , or wars , or disease, and that this is the true cause of poverty in the world in relation to real time standards that apply.

I will give you a explanation / example of this in relation to Mexico / U.S.

We have a North American free trade agreement that was enacted back in the early 1990's and that we allowed this to continue without sanctions , despite Mexico's government to not relax its own sanctions on its own people. This has caused millions of people to flee their native country due to the greed and corruption that had taken place first with their leaders and than by the U.S. leaders allowing this to continue , the result is far worse than any amount of worn torn refuges that would exile from a hostile led dictatorship in middle eastern or European countries.

The large companies that accomplish manufacturing, oil , farming , mineral extraction , automobile manufacturing get rich from tax breaks , instead of the people that need it society turns corrupt out of survival or some other profit motivated ideal, and the poor get more poor, and more exploited , until civil unrest takes place and turns there country into a place that is so screwed up , it will be many years before it can be straightened out if at all possible. This is now taking place in Mexico and has been for some time. The Mexican government is no longer able to cope with this current problem. Mean while the population is growing, the inflation will become tremendous , and the government will not be able to contain the situation, the back lash is now felt in the U.S.

There was a buffer for the people of Mexico pre the U.S. economic housing construction / real estate crisis, in that Mexicans working in the U.S. were sending billions of dollars per year to their relatives in Mexico, this was actually subsidizing the Mexican economy. When that was traumatically cut , the backlash was felt in Mexico. Many people out of rebellion to government ruling corruption turned to unsubstantiated banking practice's, narco traffic, kidnapping , murder , and so on. With 10 million Mexicans living in the U.S. and by-lingual banking agents in the U.S. there became a flood of homes , workers , drugs , ect. in the U.S. At this time a big domino scenario took place.

I am not taking about the false effect that the U.S. political so-called experts speak of but a very real economic one that has devastated the U.S. and Mexico working class. When things like this take place there is only one group that is responsible and its not any ethnic variety, it's the political process that governs the U.S. and Mexico, they could care less about the people and as long as they make a profit its well , like they say its all good . The mentality of their substantiations for their tactics is in credible.

They claim that they need the money so they can supply the work and jobs for the people that is so far from the truth it sickens me every time I here it. How is it possible to get a chicken if you have no eggs, would somebody explain that Id really like to have a good laugh, is there some kind of political process that enables the rich governments of the world to be able to lay eggs. U.S. and Mexican Presidents / congress's have been getting away with this for the last 50 years or more.

The undermining and dumbing down of society must stop not just because it is immoral the fact is that it has reached a critical point , and that a major upheaval is going to take place if it does not stop, than the whole thing will come apart.

50

A complete and devastating economic failure will occur and that's when things get real nasty. There are some sick minded people in this world that would love it when such things go on, I do not want my grandchildren to have to go thru such a thing they don't deserve that , they are not greedy bastards interested in making money at the cost of innocent people. My father did not risk his life and work hard for 70 years just to give it up and have it rolled over by such insane ideals. We all owe him and the veterans of WWII , though there are not many of them still alive. We owe it to their memory, and our own future, and or our grand children to stop this madness. If we don't one thing is for sure its going to get worse.

When the American revolution had taken place , we established guidelines so this would not happen again , what happened ? history is repeating itself if nobody has noticed. The Mexicans had there version when they stopped the Spanish, well its repeating for them as well. Our constitution stipulates that it is our duty as citizens to defend the constitution , against any thing that would undermine or compromise its intention , and it is very general, clear , & concise in its description.

 It is not vague , or ambiguous , it does say anywhere that if some one has made a loop hole they get to do what they want. The definition is based on its original cannon , there's no mention that if some one is real smart at being corrupt or if there are a group of real smart elected officials that are smart at being corrupt, they can do what they want. However the distortions have gone on , and that they might have even been voted into effect by half the people that make up this country. If that is what went on then half the people in this country are ignorant , or traitors.

It still does not make it OK , I don't care what was voted on in the legislature and what so called laws were passed . James Wilson nominated by George Washington , served in office 10-5-1789 to 8-21-1798 published a document that all authority is denied to the

British Parliament over the colonies. He was known to be the most learner of the framers of the constitution, not un-like the definition's that Samuel Adam's brought forward ,in that he was appointed associate justice of the supreme court.

He served in the military as 4th Battalion Brigadier General of the State Militia he was not a so called properly educated politician, and that his peers tried to use such mention against him , and failed.

There was a attempted lynching by a group of opposing conservative leadership , that did not like the idea that he was up holding , the constitution , and defining treason for what it was, in that poverty , inflation , food shortages and corruption was on the rise from certain party members, (does this sound familure) a group of supporters defended him at his house where this took place , the site is a national memorial now known as Fort Wilson   Note: see James Wilson (disambiguation) Wikipedia Encyclopedia.

There are 2 ways a amendment is passed , in the senate or by the states. It does not mention that if corruption was used it is acceptable. It does however by James Wilson mention that the will of the people should take precedence. After all our independence was based on sighting corruption for what it was and then declaring independence from such corruption. General Wilson almost lost his life to a domestic enemy that tried to under mind the constitution . There for it is our duty to seek out this misalignment of rules as our founding fathers did. It should also be mentioned that the British were allowed to go a long way before it was found completely intolerable to continue as it was, and that there were many disorders noted before complete independence was a forced issue out of survival for the people of the United Sates.

 In that the revolution that had taken place was mostly contrived , eventually by common citizens and not some kind of great armed force of trained soldiers that the British used against our citizens to

try and keep them subdued. These things all came to pass because
of taxes and sanctions that were imposed between class's of U.S. /
British officials running this country at that time.

All taxes paid to the U.S. are suppose to be deposited into the
Treasury , and used for the defense and the further perfection of the
United States. Our current administration has failed miserably at
their job , except for taking care of themselves, they were quite
successful at that ,while the rest of the country went to Hell. This
country was not defended properly, nor has it been improved
and or did relations with other country's achieve a reasonable effect
that benefits the United States.

 This country and all other country's that are motivated to achieve
a democracy must form a committee with the power and insight to
change the failing system into what it originally stood for, and that
the people that are supporting that country ,the working class need
to have the power to do such a thing , it is there country, they are
the ones that worked and died for it, built it , ect.

The government is the manager, not the owner, if the managers are
not performing there jobs, they must be replaced by competent
technicians , that are capable. The constitution was amended
several times to take into consideration the added situations and or
problems that would arise or become more complex due to
population , materials , or neighboring country's that would make it
a requirement.   Fair enough, it does not mean that it is manipulated
to accomplish the desires of the few and cause the mass's to suffer.
I can only stress this point so many different ways but it all spells
the same equation.

Chapter 5   A Hypocrisy feeds the corruption

Civil Actions / Policies have been responsible for the collapse of trade and dialog that would have otherwise transpired if one side or the other of the negotiating country's would have not been so dead set or ignorant of the others needs or policies that were immediately contemplated. This happens when one of the country's does not want to engage in dialog that must be contemplated.

This is required for many different reasons and that no country should be pushed into a situation rendering everything else besides that situation as scraped. This destroys the working / continual process of maintenance that is required to develop such relations. There must be a natural and non explosive or destructive way that Ideals are negotiated and expounded onto.

There is no country that has the right to make a fast judgment call onto the other with out trying to establish a working diplomacy first, and that diplomacy must be exercised until completion by the non aggressive and mature individuals that are suppose to be responsible for having such wisdom. It is not up to the presidents of these country's to determine when , and what form of dialog , or when to stop such dialog when it comes to making decision's concerning taxes and or trade / tax's between 2 country's .

These are not life and death or immediate national security issues. they are lively hood issue's, and future developments that are required based on past developments that the working people / common business's are in gagged with on a daily basis. It needs to be up to the people to be the experts in such matters because they are, the ones that are working and developing , the condition's that are being exercised. If there's anything that needs to be done immediately it is accommodating the needs of the people that are trying to work thru the basic requirements of trade , goods being transported , sold , or achieved by two country's so as the disadvantaged people are given a break to get such things to transpire. However this is not the case , and the poor are made to suffer while the wealthy / big company's conduct there business un hindered. There is a job that the wealthy and powerful companies need to do that is very hard work, there called special interested groups. It is there explicit and never ending job to try and influence the law makers / political individuals to form policy's that suite there economic needs , or desires, in a legitimate representation of coarse.

From what I have seen it has transpired very manipulatively by the powers in control of economic policy's between various country's. This is the policy of how A Hypocrisy feeds the corrupt, or should I say this is how corruption develops a hypocrisy within a country's political structure. They are one in the same and the end result is of the 2 meaning's joined in holy wedlock for better or for worse, for richer and always richer , and if some one dies they could care less its just business.

Yes it sounds pretty sick doesn't it , not as sick as the poor innocent men, women , and children that have to suffer because a group of sick ass holes cant think of doing something more creative than choking the life out of their own people, that's the really sick part.

The United States has a responsibility to the rest of the world we come up with all these products that everybody uses and enjoys , and for the most part it enables certain country's to become more productive , ect. How ever with that we have demonstrated why we are able to achieve such success. We have shown a example weather we meant to or not. However we did mean to, and there's no going back from it or trying to hide it nor should we. I was taught that if you do something you should do it right so you have some self esteem about your self. Is that not the idea, so why is it that the political process doesn't adhere to this it's the most important institution that could do the most good for the most people if they did.

The answer is personnel profit for the leaders they want to get what they feel they deserve, and that there idea is the best one, and that the good people like them will be better off if they all stick together regardless if there are innocent casualties.

They see it as unfortunate but necessary or its to bad but it could not be helped or some other lame excuse that with there so called wisdom they have forced onto everyone effected. I think that these people need to hope , they need to hope that there is not a just God that see's and remembers everything, because if there is they might not do well on there judgment day. However in the meantime people that suffer are not getting fair judgment in this life time.

 I have personally witnessed the oppression and the un-fairness of what I am speaking of. The mentality and undermining by the powers that run country's is amazing as to how they attain , on a daily basis. I have family members that live in a border town / tourist area that I have been going to on vacation's and working in and around for over 40 years it's a 1 hour drive below San Diego Calif.

General income that the public is mostly forced to except, is pathetic and that the people complaining of the food costs, should be glad to pay $5.00 a gal. for milk, so the local news caster says on a Mexican TV station. We are taking about a place that's a 1 hr. drive from San Diego Calif. one of the most valuable areas of real estate in the United States , and that this area has a construction economy that is mostly due to wealthy Americans buying property thru U.S. Banks operating in these area's,   Northern B.C.S. Mexico.

 This is no way comparable to Africa, but I guess that was the best excuse that the politico could give on national television for why thing's were not is bad as what the general public was , complaining about. I don't think I have witnessed a more subdued and undermined society, compared with the reality of what was really taking place, and who was making the money. The thing is its been that way for a long time.

There government has only privatized , most of the large corporations in the last 30 years, and the amount of corruption , tax breaks , fiscal responsibility for the wealthy is just incredible , and makes the U.S. corporations / companies look like Angels, so if you put that in perspective, it is quite incredible what you can do in that country if you have some cash.

I wont go into the other forms of corruption that takes place there, I could write a complete novel on that subject alone, although I probable would not live very long if I did , if that gives you an idea of the scope of that area that could be covered. By the way I am not a Mexican nor do I have any Hispanic heritage. My parents were U.S. and Egyptian nationals.

There's a really good reason why so many people immigrate to the U.S. its not that where they come from is a bad place , in fact people from the U.S. go to such places on vacation and would love to live in such places if they could make a living. I had such a privilege when I was younger and it was truly amazing. The problem is that most of the equipment , and supply's that are required in these place's come from the U.S. and its expensive to import , and transport , and so on, it is perfectly suited for totalitarianism.

So these people don't have a chance to do anything but live in poverty, or have to turn to an illegal way of making money out of survival although I don't condone nor have I participated in such endeavors. These countries don't have the industrial society's that the U.S. have but come on, its right next door if the rich people / governments would lighten up a little, and take the choker of the people the people would develop the country. That's how it works, who ever says it is the other way around is full of it. Do politicians build planes , boats , truck's, houses , ? no. Do they work on ranches, are they fisherman , do they work in a sweat shop ? no , yet they enjoy the product's that result from poor under paid people that do. It has to come from some where, it does not come out of the air. Even the rich peoples money has to come from somewhere, and it does it comes from poor people that work hard.

It would be very simple to basically solve most of the worlds economic problem's if you could first take out government hypocrisy. That would be the first and most important step. The next step would be to eliminate working conditions that left the workers on the verge of bankruptcy, due to unfair wage and taxation of what little is earned. Its not the workers fault that the owner of a business misrepresented himself or was not qualified to run such a business unsuspecting to the workers , or any other misuse , and exploitation of people.

 Big business has a insurance capability for product liability incase of something that happens that would cause them to be put in harms financial path. Corporations have specific rules that apply to these measures. There are specific laws that will cause people to liable for just about every type of endeavor. Just think about all the different insurance laws. How come there is not a insurance that protects the worker from people with lots of money that ambiguously start a business with out being responsible to the worker if things don't go as planned, it should be a law.

 Big companies make enough profit to pay such a premium , it would be nothing in comparison to all the other fess and process's that are paid by a business to be legally conducted.

There's only one reason such a thing doesn't take place. If workers had a fair shot at life, it would scare the people that hold power very dear to themselves for a financial reason.

In order for a higharcy to take place and be rendered successful
some one must do the work. The nature of business in most cases
does not get financially better as a company gains size / age. There
are many retirement , medical , and product liability's that are
developed because of these factors. But the most scary thing
to big business is the idea that a small and innovative company
would be on the rise , this is the scariest of all factors. A small
company is efficient , it does not have a big overhead , it is young
and does not have a lot of debt with failed strategies and or wasteful
spending because everybody wants to get there's.

As a company gets larger it must constantly grow in its capability to
sustain as it gets larger and older, however this is not always
accomplished , for many different reasons, greed and lack of future
planning are 2 main reasons. Or it is impossible do to the nature of
the company buissnes. An Example is a Airline it is economically a
bad long term ides unless a very smart long term plan is put and
kept in place. However vested interest's / stock holders demand
performance , and often this is out of desperation and not wisdom.

This leads to moral and technical short coming's, and that the
company's begin to erode from the inside out.

A smart business person will understand that things have gotten out
of hand and try to sell or make the best of a situation that is
deteriating. If you do nothing this is the final straw that will break
its back, and that it will sink because of its weight and burden.
Insurance and options would be wisely examined before it got out
of hand , because after irreversible damage occurs, its to late
and all the other business begin to circle the lame duct waiting to
move in and make the kill, its very animalistic. This is how the
strong prey on the week, no mercy just circle and strike.

The nature of higharcy works the same way I' am afraid , however nobody talks about it. When things get desperate for the floundering company it gets desperate for the workers as well, and the circling sharks know it everything's up for grabs cheap.

Technician's , labor , finance rate's , equipment , and best of all the competition is going away oh happy day.

OK so that's the break's , that's how it goes , o well , 2 bad. Wait a minute how bad does it get , maybe bad enough for the worker's in any such field to say I have had enough of this, I need to find real work. I better change my occupation , and they do , or at least they have to try or die, those are the 2 option's in this scenario what if there to old , or not smart enough , or not being paid completely devastated them into a state of financial failure, a thousand other things that could transpire because they dedicated their life to a cause and that it just got flushed down the toilet after 20 years of servitude.

There must be a fair and compensational way to insure that the innocent don't get hurt. Well there is such a country its called England, and they have such programs for financial / medical assist that insures that its subject's are not cast out onto the street with nothing.

There is a ironic joining of relation between a country of origination /exploitation , of programs and government and or financial system's you must notice the subtleties and how situation's have been played off each other for motivating purpose's.

I will give a example that starts off with England in that I feel a need to elaborate on the mentioning that a given scenario be put in proper perspective and that it will be taken from approx. 1000 years ago to the present

Example #1. Lets say because it's true that the country of England has a history of education , that promotes diversity, international trade / business, religious integrity / charity and that instead of you being hindered and looked down to like they do in a lot of country's you are up held and even promoted by colleges and for reasons that are based on one person helping another when possible . Remember these are basic principles that are exercised by the masses. When this Ideal is exercised it is successful and all the people of certain societies are benefiting and the industry thrives because of it.

But no matter what nobody gets devastated if things don't work out no matter what is striven for. Well guess what it works , and its been working for a long time. Take into consideration that the most technologically advanced , system of Aerospace , computer , medical , entertainment , ect. are all based on the English language.

The English language is the worlds No. 1 used language, and is taught in every country in the world as a second language. It's not because of some dumb reason its because the English started the process , they are the origin , it's there language , there culture their heritage.

The main theme that is taught and considered the main principle of their democracy is equality , integrity , nobility , and the quest to go out onto the world and understand it , learn from it , learn different thing's , about different people , and cultures. This obviously did not hurt or hinder their ability to prevail when thing's looked very bad. In fact they demonstrated under pressure that when they stick together, they will prevail even under great odds that would say it is not possible.

Well these principles are also what a successful business plan would be based on. It is mimicked by certain cultures that are extremely successful per capita. France, Germany , Japan to name the most successful , there are others in Northern Europe, and Asia.

Accountability and conservatism is the key to success in putting a system together that meet's economic , and society need's of the population. After a basic outline is fully defined features can be added or deleted to further perfect or enable a positive growth scenario. Integrity must be constantly maintained , so that corruption cannot gain a foot hold. This is done more easily when a society is smaller , however when there are individual states , this becomes a national burden , and that regional efforts must be supported and maintained.

This adds buracrocity however the basic plan of fiscal performance is still the same if maintained fairly and proportionally and does not need to be forfeited or compromised if this is allowed to happen as it has in places like Washington D.C. , Mexico city D.F., and other capitol city's thru out the world. These place's have enacted sub-cultures that they don't want the poor people to access.

They really believe that they are above being controlled or regulated and for the most part they are beyond being regulated. Even if they were they would find away around the rules, they are quite intelligent at such tactic's.

The solution is simple , its what our laws are based on, and the result of their action's. They need to be accountable for their actions , immediately, not 2 ,4, or 5 years from now when they have already succeeded at devastating the poor. Now means right now as soon as you have become aware. Just like the rules for a civil or criminal action , the policy is very plane. Responsibility and or constituted action is based on when you first become aware of the actions that are or have taken place. If the government is not working at a efficient enough rate , than maybe a private company would be better suited or qualified to do the job, or a recall is in order but to do nothing and allow the mistakes and failures to continue is the worst thing that could take place.

That's how it works anyway, why wait get the best people on it now if there is a big problem and the government is not able to handle it or there to busy, or what ever there problem is. Laws and the implementation of laws and policies should be based on the immediate requirement to enact them. If you wait to do so disaster is the result weather it has to do with physical , mental , and or financial.

Since when in the history of recorded history has the wait and see method of dealing with impending discourse and or suspected fault been the policy in the case of a emergency rectification every led to anything but disaster. U.S. intelligence personnel first responders need to have a office in Washington , and I' am not talking about special elite warrior forces that are specially trained to combat a bunch of crazy nuts , in old Toyota pickup trucks high on heroin , shooting their AK-47's in the air, thousands of miles away from the U.S.

What is far more dangerous is the effect of domestic policy corruption. If anyone has been paying attention those policy's have fed the rhetoric that the people with the pick up trucks , that are high on heroin have been using against the world to further their cause.

If I did not know better based on what I have been seeing there are people in Washington D.C. that seem to be on heroin or something, they move so slow and are so mentally handicapped the comparison is amazing. I think current politicians should have drug testing , seriously !!. They don't do much to stop the trade maybe their hooked ? . I don't know for sure if they are on drug's but they are very screwed up, and there is not much of a difference in the way they work compared to their adversary's , with the exception of their attire , wealth , and living accommodation's.   Its just amazing.

Chapter 6   Blind leaders don't want you to see

The so called self proclaimed educated leaders that run countries are
not any where close to being qualified to accomplish such a thing
successfully for the most part , and that such occurrence's only had
taken place on a limited basis, thru out recorded history. A lot of
times when it had taken place successfully, it was looked at as a
special occurrence instead of the normal method that always
was needed on a constant basis.

  Revolution's were for the most part what changed the standard
order of corruption. Today however because of population growth
and world wide media access, the role's of change are taking
different paths to the result.   It is very unfortunate that the young
or innocent are paying the price for their leaders failed policies and
or Ideal's.

The Human race is being cheated , manipulated , misrepresented ,
exploited , deprived , by the blindness of arrogance , oppression ,
waste , and limited materials, that have resulted from
mismanagement by leader's. Management system's /
organization's are not concerned with reality because it is not their
reality. It's someone else's and that they feel it is up to the people
to straighten things out and that they merely need to point them in
the right direction, and the rest is up to the force's wishing to
prevail .

 How can they be so irresponsible to say, and do such things with
our valuable resources the young, the strong , our futures , their
future's . This is the year 2008 there is not much that is not known
about anything weather it has to do with physic's , atomic energy ,
medical , and more than easily enough politics and the results of
policies. So who's kidding who, I know who's trying to brain wash

64

me do you. If it was up to corrupt leaders they would have us all rounded up , marched into a pit and smothered out of existence, or better yet they get us to smother ourselves .

They call it ethnic cleansing , or some other excuse for genocide , and it goes on every day even in civilized country's by people giving the appearance that only civilized actions are taking place and or killing's that are going on ,in the most humane way possible.

This is how deranged leader's deal with 'their problems , pure ignorance , and greed. A leaders job is to lead if he does not , than his job cannot be justified. He must find a way to lead in a time of critical situation's and that if he does not understand how to do this properly he will have to invent a form right or wrong.

Most of the leaders don't have this knowledge or wish to demonstrate diplomacy ,because if they had acted fairly than people would understand that a confrontation out of desperation for anything but a immediate defense is not the proper form of policy. They would have carefully and thoughtfully carried out policy's that were the most intelligent form of mediation and or plot strategies that due not leave the innocent as the ones to suffer , this almost never takes place.

Plain and simple most leaders are hacks and they shoot from the hip , except for Dick Chaney he uses a rifle with a scope and he still cant see well enough as to not shoot his own friends and mistake them for duct's. With their Ideals , and lack of respect / care and preparation , & planning for defensive or offensive successful policy's. To engage protesting and causing of cultural revolutions have need to be enacted because of repression and irresponsibility for life that render society's helpless.

At that point the Idea of nobody stepping forward to lend assistance to what is needed is being neglectful to the extent of non participation when the proper response would have been to demand account ability for such conditions. That would be the responsible time to deal with a given scenario of dealing with any corrupt or negligent leadership issues or factors. Compromise should not be an excuse for doing nothing, it is death , it promotes failure , you cant go any further.

The elders in society that are real human beings know they have a duty to for fill if at all possible, and that is to enlighten the young people to be hopeful and exert themselves, and teach them to not settle for ignorance of the truth. This is suppose to go on, it is why people have kids its their responsibility. If you live somewhere or work for someone that promotes nothing than you owe your self to be free of such oppression at least in your mind so you can plan on making a alternative occur as soon as possible.

If truth and true knowledge can not replace a hoax and or expose corruption one in the same in a lot of case's than what can be done to improve the situation, well the answer is basically nothing because nothing will change at that point and no ones going to be going forward.

Its real simple , if you have wood rot its got to go. If you have theory it has to be proven, if it doesn't work you have to recognize the reason why , like it or not. More times than you would think possible there's been a tremendous amount of hype , advertising , trend manipulation , media displacement, and distortion of the truth. Make no mistake their not this is there stock and trade to guide you and make you buy what's being sold and to actually convince you that it is your duty to buy in.

There is only one thing that pays a media company and that's client's and advertiser's . So when they say why ask why just try Bud Dry, they have said it all. The base of the content is not relevant I don't care how nice or sincere they appear on TV you have to see thru this or they have gotten thru they brain washed you and your done.

66

I don't dislike hype I just want it to have some integrity, and or substance. The ignorance makes me want to throw a brick at the TV and I just cant afford it. If I had money to buy a lot of TV's , I would make a show about why I killed my TV , and it's theme would be if you haven't guessed , showing clips of the most useless , brainwashing dumbing up of society crap that was out on the airwaves, the finally would be throwing a brick thru the TV at the lame clip that was being shown so that people would get it , that there being hyped to death as a society. People need to take control kill your TV don't be afraid I'm not. I started destroying TV's when I was young I loved to watch them implode after tossing a rock or brick at them, normally these TV's were no longer functional, that being the prime reason for the destruction. People would just put them in their trash can at the end of the week , and then the trash man would get all the fun of killing it with his enormous trash compacting shoveling trash truck that sounded like a dying prehistoric animal.

I don't know why I am like this I used to here my father sometimes say when he was watching TV , what a bunch of Fing Jack Ass's , for that matter he used to call me one when I did something stupid. So I guess I inherited it because that's what I say, when I see something totally lame on TV. I haven't destroyed a TV in at least 36 years. I guess it's the law that they must be recycled these days. Don't get me wrong its not the TV that my father and I hated it's the content that it displayed sometimes. I think it is legal in Nevada, they stock pile nuclear waste there maybe they wouldn't mind if I broke just one there.

The point is that if what the responsible people are trying to say, is not responsible or innovative than they are producing a hoax. The hoax is contrived as part of a master plan of ideal shaping and influence to give society's the idea , everything is just fine if you buy in , and get a long with there way of seeing things. The scary thing is that they might be buying into their own propaganda , or that they are accurately reflecting their true character. Regardless it is extremely difficult to not be affected by outside influence's either directly on a daily basis or subliminally and not known to you, even if you are consciously trying to not be affected.

When people are confused by things, it tends to make them mentally immobilized. This is also part of the plan to promote stress and brain immobilization in that nobody understands what happened . Believe me somebody does know what happened. For the most part the News media in all societies are guilty of the negative and overwhelming effect of sensational pictures, sites , and sounds. However a lot of the times they do display accurately depicted information , but when they are in the dumbing up mode people revert back subconsciously as to the validity or integrity of what they are seeing. It is inconsistent that this also effects people that are not able to go back and forth the way professional mind control experts move in this area effortlessly. I would like to site what I believe to be the most prolific example that being in my mind the fox news channel , and all the non-cable primary station's CBS , NBC , ABC.

There have been some very well made documentary's that have come out in the past few years , explaining the system I am speaking of, and I would advise seeing and investigating documentary's and historical event's , that transpired .
I knew of some of the information from personally witnessing or being involved. To see my interpretations up held by others makes me think that it gives me a better self assurance that its not me, and that what's going on really is taking place and that I am not interpreting it inaccurately. This has everything to do with the facts of any policies being examinable, and we should be able to have a review of the integrity of such perception's, with out a impiousness that would cause anything but the truth to be shown, as the relevance of a event. If Government institutions put the money they made from corruption of a society into the construction of the innocent's needs it would take because it is geared for growth, and the people that wanted to be part of that would begin to form a sub-

culture that was not comprised of the corrupt, for the most part and it would be easily deciphered.

Civil terror (armed killing crimes) in the United States has been recorded to cost more than war. For the year of 2007 the combined cumulative loss attributed to violent crime was approx. 45 Billion Dollars for that year alone as a 162 page report that our government put out. Those are direct result costs , courts , lost investment , bank loss's , police , prisons , ect. At the same time no money is being spent on a intelligent way of stopping such desperation , almost all of these crimes involved fire arms.

If sub-cultures were maintained , with intelligence that was not misguided or forgotten there would be a reason behind it, people maintaining the integrity of such programs could identify the guilty factions that were undermining such a effort. The proper coordination of a facilitation to maintain order and non-corruption would take precedence. To deal with any problem effectively there must be motivation, and I don't mean by fear ,because this only promotes more fear and or corruption.

Proper motivation is much less money maybe a thousand times less than the extreme use of force that only comes and goes and than the process starts again of corruption infiltration. So from a economic stand point you can not shoot enough criminals , because you will run out of money first, and the only thing that will be accomplished is more corruption and civil strife.

Society drives the sociopath personality , the drugs and mind altering chemicals only make a more complex situation that exists, regardless. Getting someone clean helps but it does not solve the problem as to why it exists. It is a cultural / social problem and that to truly dissolve it you must have a stronger remedy than the cause. This is only developed by the furtherance and upholding of humanism. There must be a clear and concise plan for people to have hope and desire to do the right thing. They are lured and

seduced easily to take the easy degenerative routes , this form of
society support and preponderance must stop , and starts by our
leaders stopping and acknowledging they have a problem and then
implementing a creditable solution , that is community based.

There is no easy button for dealing with such problems. The only
reality is intelligence its not going to work any other way. If people
are going to behave like animals, you must deal with that specific
problem and cause the packs to split and dissolve until they are
regionally displaced , contained , or illuminated by proper selection
and not any amount of guessing or unproven theory.

 This is best accomplished with Intel. because you must replace
failure with success , and success must be maintained, it does
not just grow on a tree. The people in the world that are specialist's
in being intelligent did not accomplish such a thing as easy as it is
required to form corruption / destruction.

Anytime success takes hold it is because people get behind it. The
basis for such a ideal must be maintained , and considered more
important than anything else, and that many worked hard , and that
there was a lot of times much sacrifice for such things that did take
place. If we cannot at least honor the ideal of the sacrifice,
we have failed as a non-corrupt culture. I am not taking about
giving someone a medal or building a monument, but real honor
by carrying thru with the intention of those that ultimately sacrificed
for such ideals of non-corruption , to try and take hold.

It should not be of the mentality if a leader is judged that his
misgivings are interpreted by an opinion , if non performance is a
result , it his responsibility , above all others for his neglect and or
comprehension lack of ,for him or his subordinates and that
he must be held accountable for allowing his subordinates to
produce a more pronounced lack of comprehension or performance

that would take place. I have just given you a example of the
federal code of regulations , that are required to be enforced
in every federally approved system of organization.   Organizations
that have demonstrated failure to comply are issued billions of
dollars each year in fines.

Those same organizations that have been found negligent were
required to dismiss technicians / personnel from their positions , at
or within that organizations structure and or society of work related
industry. This is considered a world standard that
most of the free world country's exercise. It is a system that the
United States has championed in the past , and proved to be the
most successful industrialized country in the world to achieve its
level of status / comprehension.

This was always done so as it is presently , in all political speeches
made by our current leaders ,and past / founding fathers of the
United States system, on the basis for the drafting of the
constitution ultimately, that God was the supreme reason and
knowledge behind the self evident truths that would manifest from
such policy's.

Well that's saying a lot , if that's your country's motto. It also is
printed on our monetary form , there for given all that , their can be
little doubt what the intension of the United States Policy stands for.

If we do not exercise our country's policy with continues planning
for uninterrupted performance of the policy than it is a failed policy
and must be terminated immediately, before anyone else could
possible be hurt or bodily injured. This is a federal law that
takes precedence for issuance in the case of an emergency.
If the same laws that apply for the civil sector of a country are not
enforced onto federal appointed employees this is illegal and
everyone involved in such undermining is guilty and subject to in
the case of a government official. It is grand treason for ultimate
lack of responsibility to occur knowing so and actually plotting,

71

and carrying thru with such policy that became self evident as a result.

The Idea that a federal official is exempted of civil law practice's displays a flaw in the system , this must be addressed immediately it is the law, to enforce integrity onto large or small government ran operation's.

The U.S. military is in the operation of a rule book extension of statues. All though it is supposed to operate in accordance with the federal codes of procedure, that are considered pertinent to that entity , nevertheless it is a entity / operational system that is physically taking place, and that it is subject to use or non use in the case of an immediate emergency. This does not give it the authority to do what ever it wants.

From a leaders point of view for one very important law, the President is considered the commander and chief above all and any other description of duties of the President. This is his / her top duty description , and that his / her subordinates , generals , soldiers ect. are held to standards of responsibility equal to most civil laws. So why would that policy not apply to the President, and at what point from somebody's wise opinion does it change, at his cabinet, where do you separate the highharchy from the lower harchy. I would like to know this I am very curious. If there was such a law, I find it to undermine the constitution , and expose it as a error or flaw that must be corrected , to stay within the scope of the United States non-corrupt policy. It would also apply that by definition of the constitution that a corruption of blood clause would be enforced where applicable and that a individual found guilty due to that degree would have his or hers and or any part of their family or association of any part of, to be deigned any such monetary gain or property, from acts proven to be the result of misconduct, and or the cumulative worth of any such individual, that was found guilty of such a crime.

The United States has been on record to enforce such actions , as the result of hostile or corrupt / incompetent individuals and or corporation's. There has been Billions of dollars spent by tax payers for the enforcement of these laws. Between the Billions spent on enforcement and Billions collected in fines. There is not a budget for the innocent victims that are compelled to testify to such things or be held for obstruction or contempt of the law. If they did not with the exception of the witness protection plan and or a state bar attorney miss conduct insurance fund.

These programs do not compare in relation to the real world scenario, they are completely not proportional in relation to what the cost is to the participating individuals , in upholding the principle of law.   Why are they not compensated proportionally , why are our military personnel that served and have made some of the most noble stands for democracy not compensated or cared for proportionally.

What I am trying to say is that our leaders get away with murder and all the subjects have to pay.   I am sorry but this is how ants exist, they all work for the queen ant just to build that pile of sand up for the queen ant to be carried up to the top of the pile to glance over her kingdom when ever she feels like it and that's it ,there's nothing else. Life exists like that for the ants they never evolve, they have been ants for millions of years , its just the story of the ants.

Our constitution says its origin is constructed because of the principles of a just and fair God, well folks if God made everything including the ant's were not saying much if we immulate ants as a society as far as our basic policy's go. Other than insulting God these leaders ,having done worse than merely insulting anything, the United States is responsible for the financial markets of the world. That's because the rest of the worlds banks, have financed failed policies , and wasteful spending, that came from the private , and government institutions.

When the U.S. fails so does the rest of the world is effected. This causes a tremendous global problem and lead's to economic problems with the country's that have a vested interest.

If the United States does not set a moral and economic example of solvent policies the world will decline in the quality of life and or expected containment of resources required to for fill population expansion. The amount of economic , environmental, and moral non-solution's to the population increase will over burden the world. At some point a breaking point will occur that will cause overwhelming inflation.

When George Orwell predicted moralistic upheaval for 1983 , he only touched on problems in comparison to what will happen starting in 2010. All the results of today's problems come from the result of industrialization non performance in conjunction with fair pricing , adjustment for population / inflation. This is due to greed ,incompetence , non-realistic or conducive business practice.

This is a declining spiral that will cause further destabilization of the world markets and resource capability. Company's that have outsourced there needs will not be able to for fill there requirements eventually civil unrest , disease, and shortages in areas that have extreme weather conditions equatorial regions that normally receive support from the Northern or Southern less volatile areas will be unable to afford to assist those areas at a price that is realistic.
This will lead to the furtherance of disease and civil unrest. These factors will eventually effect the North or Southern areas from the equator in extreme way's. We are already feeling this effect in the United States , from the result of Mexico , and Central America, the only thing that makes things not as bad as the effects felt in Europe is the fact that Central America is very small in contrast to the equivalent Geographic effects that are based out of Africa / middle east regions.

The price of fuel and materials in Europe have always been much higher than those in the U.S. , this has everything to with the civil problems verses non planning of extreme events in marketing and banking that is more inclined to rely on the U.S. to take up the slack and or buffer because they have been doing this for a long time.

It is a established trend for the past 60 years that the U.S. could afford to intervene and that 60 years ago it was financially lucrative to do so. That's because of a decreased population underdeveloped world capability and that everything was produced industrially for a large part by the U.S. . This is no longer the case, however traditional profit expectance has not realistically been changed to reflect 2010 world scenario, and that at this point the world has not prepared for the eventuality, of what's to come. Things are very complicated now there is no possible way things can continue the way they started.

If the world does not take them selves seriously there will be worse problems before a breaking point / financial complete failure occurs. At that point there will be a multitude of other associated failures that will also occur, the world is feeling the effects now that are beginning to take place.

Thru out History the result of blindness to such facts have caused the worst effects that have ever been recorded by History. The middle ages (dark ages), WWI , WWII , mish . other world conflict's . They were all caused by mismanagement, greed , and ignorance of the result from not planning on the events that inevitable always followed. Not being prepared , is not a acceptable excuse. The results are because of the facts of physics' and are undisputable , as to the origins cause's.

At this point in time as far as I can see with my eyes open the leaders / adult's of the world are acting like children , and closing there eyes , and hoping all the bad goes away. So does that mean the kids have to be responsible ? its sure is looking that way.

Make no mistake my young friend's , if you don't organize intelligently, your elder leader's are going to screw you so bad you wont ever get over it , your life means something don't let them convince you other wise , step up tell them to go F them self not you , don't take the bait they put in front of you , don't except there reason's, show some back bone and take control of your destiny I promise you will be glad you did.

 Your friends and peers will admire you for being different , define your life's axis to be as bold as your love for life, and remember one thing your only young once , but you will live in many different stages of life's level's.

Chapter   7   How the Phoenix fly's

When ever a society based system fails it leaves all the broken parts
in there, as is condition . Next some one uses the corruption that
settles in to take advantage of the situation. There's always some
kind of benefit towards the development of corruption that occurs.
It start's out normally by a aggressive military type of force that
take's the situation to a point of there desires being realized and
enhanced thru fear and regime status.

 Once this occurs it attracts the interest of someone wanting to
utilize such type's of a force in any particular geographic
location , and that various plan's to use and or exploit the local
situation is planned and executed with calculation for the various
factors considered.

The thing that is conducive for such scenarios deals with the fact
of it not being a concern what the local environment has to offer, in
that this type of situation does not normally occur in area's that
don't have exploitable reasons to invest the time in doing such a
thing and that , planning is normally contemplated by the aggressor
that started such a mess in the first place.

A continues loop effect is always in effect where these condition's
would prevail , that's because they would be located in mostly non
desirable area's
that are diseased , and or have marginal supply capability to sustain
a society. In a lot of case's these places might have started out as
humanitarian based efforts and that once established , the aggressive
presence would come onto the scene and assert its goal's and
persistence. Because of political and or logistical non support of a
situation it is allowed to escalate. Profit is a incredible motivator in

area's that are lacking in the capability to earn money so the bad influence is taken into by local participant's and escalation of a aggressor is enhanced. The world of humanitarian aid must maintain its situational capability thru the recognizing and action required to uphold and support the investment of aid. It must be prepared to serve a double roll in aid to people. This has always been known however not taken seriously enough until escalation has taken place and the situation has developed to the next phase of its cycle.

To some it up, you help people then they rip you off , and you have to deal with this ridicules situation , and you find yourself asking why did we waist our time in the first place, well its real simple. There are a lot of people that would do nothing in the first place, and in the second place they cant wait to rub it in your face, and say see we told you , you were not going to do well.

These people had a attitude from the start, and that the only thing that ever mattered was what they were going to get out of there boring little world that consisted of the same thing everyday , never taking chance's , never trying something new , not ever putting someone else's need's before there own.

Most of these people come from a place that never had to depend on someone else to have the integrity for them to accomplish something , in combining there capability with others. Well this point is defined at the time of birth if nobody slapped your but , when you were born you might never had taken a breath or lived , but somebody cared enough to do this. Most people don't know who was responsible for them to get there first breath, however they are alive because of it, because somebody cared.

There are many emergency's that go on every day in society's all over the world where somebody cared enough so you would not have to dye needlessly at birth, or thru out the coarse of your life's history.

This is a trait that defines us as human's , we do such things because we desire to be compassionate , regardless as to what level we take such ideal's, never the less it is that we desire to do these things. Some of us would feel insignificant in not demonstrating such a cause. Maybe our parent's or someone we loved and respected was this way , and we are compelled to do so, and might even be fearful of our own subconscious by non participation.

What ever the compelling reason , the world is a better place because of such ideal's. There is more good and less bad , and that when people work together to accomplish things that define them as good and compassionate, they have a reason to be joyful , and celebrate in the greatness of there accomplishment as a society. There is rarely a better feeling someone can have in life after they have unselfishly been responsible in helping or saving a person's life , future , financial capability , a life's work , and so on. I know this from practical experience I had done this on many occasions thru out the coarse of my life, for other people , and that I grew up around adults that did such thing's.

I have also known the feeling of being broken, ripped off, cheated harmed , taken advantage of , bullied , stripped of all my material accomplishment's, and found my self asking but why me , I did not deserve this , where's my reward for fighting the good fight. ? The answer is I know what I am , and how I became the way I am , I have the knowledge to know the ultimate truth. This is something no amount of money can buy, no attainable status other's can give to you , because you accomplished such thing's , and they mean what they mean to you , and or the people you cared about.

This is more powerful and meaningful than anything any other person could possibly instill onto you for any reason, and best of all you have the gift of great memories that will last you your entire life.

You will not be one of those people that ask's them self's maybe I should not have turned away. Maybe I should have not been so selfish. What's strange to me is I don't have a lot of memories that , are concerning the moment's in my life where self gratitude is a pronounced memory , except for when I was a small child. For most of my adult life the memories that arise most are those when I was involved with someone being assisted from the result of my work's and effort, where there was enjoyment of a group or more than , only myself being the result of a significant endeavor.

Who knows maybe I was brain washed into being a compassionate and or over emotional person , maybe , but I did not nor did anyone else because of such ideals suffer , and that it benefited myself and other's that I was involved with such action's that had taken place.

People that have never thought this way , cannot really understand this , it is something that has to mean something to the individual that gains such perception's. Another self perception that is probably considered the most valuable of such ideal's is the effect when a person triumph's over the hopeless situation , and that out of wreckage or failure you are able to regain and start a new with nothing but your persistence that enabled you , out of the use of patience , time , humility , and or other contributing factors enabled such people to overcome, this too I know in that I had succeeded as many times as I was hindered.

I have to believe these are test's of the caliber of our humanism. Some of us are detracted from the potential of our capability's because of outside influence , this is the gravest form of ideal disruption. It is our own choice that we make for our selves as to contribute or not , to the humanism cause. There is much confusion in these type's of perception's, we desire as a society to be recognized for our accomplishment's and that sometimes this can hinder the main reason for our cause, and we can often find ourselves slipping into a realm of perception that detracts from the point of the endeavor., this is especially true when you take into consideration your immediate environment , which we are all a product of , good or bad , like it or not, the true test is to be able to shut out the distraction while you concentrate on the task at hand and continue to prevail, this is the most difficult way to attain , however it is the best test of your resolve.

I always found it pointless if I was alone in my sought endeavor's regardless as to the material gain , and that for it to be accomplished , and I being alone, it did not have the same value , I am not saying that's for everyone but I don't think I am the only one that thinks such thought's. It always made me feel more whole / alive when those around me could benefit from a endeavor that was a proud success to my self.

This is a basic human trait and weather people will admit or not many feel the same way or secretly wished they could or are even envious of those that aspired to such things, in the endeavors they perused. This is how a society can truly have pride in there immediate group of peer's. If only there were more politician's that had such aspiration's , I humbly think there would be greater things accomplished in the world. The leaders are the hope for the helpless , or the uneducated or the unable ones. The true roll of a leader should be to instruct society as to what the ultimate goals of aspiration should or could be with respect to a society's collective involvement , this builds a camaraderie that is very inspiring to the masses.

When a leader does not do this , the opposite effect is retained. The masses are disenchanted , hopelessness settles in , corruption gains a foot hold ,there is a general consensus that its OK to be a lyre , or a cheat , or other disingenuous conditions to take place within a given society. When I was a kid and I was told why I should not do things stupid, people would say things like would you jump off a cliff if some one else does , and my answer of coarse was no way. Well its amazing that grown adults would go and follow the guy in front of him and jump off that cliff , like a bunch of monkeys. I guess they drew a different meaning from such idealisms. Politician's certainly do , these days I see that they are doing the monkey see monkey do routine a lot.

One thing society must remember if they want to survive, is never let anyone make a monkey out of you. NASA could not go around the planet and return with out burning up twice. This is a direct result of a culture shift , from integrity to disregard . People would say they died doing what they loved , really I don't know anyone who would love to burn to death because someone did not want to take the time to do their job correctly that obviously did not love their job, because if they did it would have mattered more that they got it right, no matter what, and that the people that were suppose to be responsible for other people's safety failed at their job, and that it would be excusable is completely ridicules .

Such people in the NASA , and of FAA organizations should be brought up on charges of man slotter. The same goes for people that were suppose to be in charge of security at airports that let terrorist's infiltrate our system simultaneously in 4 separate occurrences at once it is obvious that the government is incapable to manage anything that really matters except how to collect tax's. They are apparently experts look how much money they collect , and how little the worker that pays the tax's earns for his efforts, I guess I am being unfair they are also experts at wasteful spending. Come to think of it they are really good at a lot of useless thing's , I guess there is a real need for government management , if we did not have examples of extreme incompetence , people would not understand the meaning of true ignorance / derelict of duty, so let that be a lesson to us, if you want something done right , you will have to do it your self or die.

Chapter   8   The Suicide Mission

Over population literally makes people fall off the side of the world it is a phenomena that actually does exist. How's that you say it defies physics , impossible .

That's right its no joke , I will explain exactly how it happens , the where , the who , and the why. The where could be anywhere , however it is a metaphoric place in relation to where a individual has been living. The events that transpired within ones perceptions of life. The who could be anyone , however we will focus on personnel of the U.S. armed forces for the example to be given.

There are literally hundreds of thousands of people that ,thru out the world each year this phenomena has transgressed onto , aside from the U. S. military personnel . The why is because nobody cared to help these people that were falling, however some of them just slipped and there was nothing that anyone could have done to stop it, at that point.

In one year , 17 U.S. veterans each day committed suicide, that's 120 per week , 6,256 a year for 2005 , and estimated to increase those amount's 10% per year to date, from PTSD (Post Traumatic Stress Disorder) caused mostly by despair , neglect from society, and poverty. 25% of all enlistees / 50% reservists come back from Iraq totally screwed up. There symptoms are night mares , flash backs , cannot hold a job, can't handle society , there are presently 800,000 cases of PTSD at this time , 6 million vets / families have no health care to deal with there problems that the U.S. government pushed onto them , 130 suicide bombers blew them selves up in 2005 (mostly Iraqi's) vs. 6,256 U.S military personnel that committed suicide in 2005 because of horrible things that they witnessed, or that they inflicted onto another humane being.

Think about this scenario you volunteer to fight the good fight , so you can provide for your family back home and defend freedom. You accidentally blow up someone's family , and you're the kind of person that has a conscious , you start thinking about the whole thing you come to the conclusion that what you did was the worst thing that you could have done. How do I fix it , you cant its been done , there's some woman and her baby all over the place in a hundred different parts all around you, I don't know about you but I would feel bad if I was responsible for such a thing.

You finish your tour , you come home your wife's found a new man she was tired of you having to make multiple tours , and wanted to get on with life. Your kids have a new daddy, and your life is not worth 2 cents in your mind, so what do you do, 6,256 brave vets had a tough time coping and decided that the whole thing was hopeless. There are estimates that show current numbers of military suicide is around 1,000 per month as of September of 2008. That's just one scenario there are thousands of different reasons why they had decided to end there life, but it was there choice , there last piece of individuality , in that everything else that was going on was not of their choice and that the responsible ones (our government) would not assist them in there time of need.

 However when the government wanted to make a profit ,they got what they wanted, at a cost to all the innocent people that were caught in the crossfire.

All the major city's in the U.S. have been stretched to their limits with people that are all trying to accomplish the same thing. Have a job , home , relationship , all the normal stuff that every one in the world wants. This is mainly due because of government greed policy's. The greed originates by non involvement of NATO , UN, and mostly standard civil policy's between the U.S. and other country's that are involved with the U.S. trade system's . Participation would solve problems in other country's so that there populations would not illegally come here to the U.S. as much as they are. This is a ongoing problem that I have witnessed for over 15 years. One administration gives them amnesty , the other punishes , they other deports , they don't know if there coming or going.

Its profitable for big business to have these problems so they think or as if they could care anyway. Its extremely difficult for people that don't understand a foreign language to just pack it up and go into the unknown with no help , education , ect.,
but they do it because they are forced into it for several particular reason's most of them not very nice ones.

My father grew up during the great U.S. depression , and as a young boy he never new his mother , and his father suffered a sever leg injury working in a steel mill and could not provide , for his family, so he resorted to making bathtub gin for the blues club's on the south side of Chicago, that's right where those black people made a living entertaining white people that had money. Thanks to those black people from New Orleans / Mississippi delta , my grand father was able to provide a meal sometimes for his family.

My father watched gangsters drive down the streets with machine guns blazing , just like in the movies except it was real. When he turned 18 he was drafted and said it was the best thing that ever happened to him, he was able to escape poverty, and gain a education from the GI bill that applied to WWII vets. He told me that for the poor people the military was one of the only ways of escaping the cycle of poverty if you wanted to make a honest living.

Today 2008 there are to many people and not enough jobs and that the military is one of the only options for many people male or female. Our government smugly knows it more so because they caused this problem. They cant blame Adolph Hitler or the Imperial rulers of Japan , two very formable aggressors that had unlimited equipment at there disposal , and highly educated and willingly brainwashed supply's of subjects to carry out the well executed tactics that were utilized at that time against the free world.

With all the technology these day's, jets, helicopters, money, resource's ect, the idea that the worlds powers cannot stop corruption of non formidable aggressors that have nothing compared to the world power's, to me is amazing, what the hell are we doing, the incompetence level must be staggering.

I don't think so, the equipment and personnel that the military utilizes today is very sophisticated, and is designed to maximize results, and the Idea that the adversary has none of this weaponry, and we cant stop them, only leads me to believe that the powerful people don't want to because it would stop the flow of money at that point.

The Ideals are the problem, we have been brain washed into thinking that fighting is good, we must, its our duty, it's the right thing to do, its fun, ect. then reality sets in, and all that you thought was right turns out to be wrong, and then its to late.

I really believe that the military should have a trade union, some kind of advocate that steps in right away and says OK hold on a minute here, things are not getting done correctly, or fairly, or safe and that everybody in the military is going on strike until things get straightened out. There's not that many people in the military these days, it's not like WWII, where every available soul is needed. there's no draft. There are more people involved in other areas of work, or close to the same type of work in the military, and they have union's. They have right's, insurance guarantee's that someone is watching there back.

For one of the most dangerous job this country has, they do not have adequate support, I don't get I'll bet the government would get there act together real quick if such a thing went on, first the military personnel would have to be assured they would not go to jail for trying to uphold the constitution. Next who would pay them in the interim, that's a little problem, but that's when it comes down to morals what's more important life or money.

Well for the banking institutions we know that money is there life , they have no problem failing and causing hundreds of billions of dollars in debt. and thinking nothing of it. These are the people that finance the world , government regulators. Someone has to step up , where's all this money coming from and where's it going its not some game its peoples lives. I don't care what religion , or race , or country you come from when a traumatic occurrence takes place like loosing everything you worked for in life , or loosing your family or your honor , if you are so inclined to have such a thing.

Your life in your mind is not worth 2 cent's , and to end your life in hope that God will give you a better one next time around occurs to some people that might believe in God. Or they might be thinking its just not worth it anymore , you try and try and only get screwed every time , or a thousand other reasons that never should have been contemplated in the first place.

All that so the rich people could stay rich and force poor people to stay poor. Not that they needed all that money that they could not spend in 1000 life times, but just to play God, because being a human being and living and working to further the cause of humanism was just not good enough. Well I hope all you cooperate / government assholes are proud of your selves. I hope I am being as insulting and negative towards you that I could possible be with out sounding like a asshole myself , or having to bring my self down to your pathetic level of corruption.

As for the victims remember its not you , its them they did this not you it was all their Idea to perpetuate things , so don't let them screw you, stand up and tell them to stick their money you know where. If enough people get behind a cause it will take , it worked in the 60's / 70's it can happen again its up to us we have the choice to win or loose against True Evil.

The suicide bombers in Iraq , Afghanistan , Saudi Arabia , Pakistan are all driven by the cause of ignorance , if the cause was illuminated they might stop . The people that they live with and infiltrate with their version of society are forced and or don't realize the extent of ignorance that is played into by all the factions pertaining. The main distraction is money, it costs money to make bombs , and buy gun's , and have equipment to persist , and just as the free world needs money to sustain , so do rebel faction's .

They also need food and materials to sustain , and that many of them are drug users and or that a lot of their capability comes from the sale of drugs. This same effect takes place in South America.

The main cause of a war must be stopped in order to stop the capability of the aggressor. When wars are fought against formable aggressors, the industrial capability's of the enemy are sought and destroyed as the priority to gain the upper hand, this was learned and common knowledge beginning with WWI, more so with WWII.

If the free world really wanted to it could solve many of it's problems at the same time buy illuminating the middle eastern drug trade and replacing it with legitimate systems of society needs for people to sustain them selves like human being's. Why not bomb and target the real enemy the drug growers and regimes that back those activities. These regimes are various countries in the middle east and that their leaders are responsible for the non economic development of their country that stems from a drug trade . This is a bigger problem than people realize not to mention a down syndrome that is genetically developed into the rebellious ones'.

You can't eat heroin they must change their culture if it is having a negative impact on people this is a humanitarian effort that would gain support of the people because it would instill a sense of hope and compassion for people that have had nothing for generation after generation except drugs , desperation , and a sick excuse for religion that is misaligned with reality, due to the effect of desperation and a constant fear of war , dictators , and generally non-support by the outside world of their true needs ,

The aggressors would have to turn to defend their precious drug trade, they would at that point expose them selves making it legitimate to target and or stop them with a minimum of collateral damage and that anyone caught up in such endeavors would be self depleting from such a system.

This can only be successful if the population is behind it , they will not get behind rhetoric and only talk, because that is what the problem comes from. Lots of people talking and few of them knowing or caring of the true problems and desperation that plagues their country.

When you play with a snake you must hold it by the head. If your aggressor is a snake you need only to bate him with the drug's they are addicted to by controlling the drug trade you are now holding him by the head. That would be the first step in stopping the aggressor and his propaganda capability.

The next is to give a exchange for support of an ideal , the needed items required to basically sustain and have further containment of a normal society system.

People that strap bombs to them selves , and then cause mayhem must be on drugs for sure , think about it ,normal people don't do those thing's normally. There might be a occasional sociopath , but those disorders are a result of mind altering condition's . However you must look past the drug inducement because it is a after effect of the nature of the true cause. That primary cause is that those people that use the drugs, do so to mask the pain and suffering of a repressed life, that they see no hope for, this is a sociopathic condition that has a effect on everyone in a particular region that struggles to get thru life each day. Just take a look at the gang bangers in the repressed city's that are located in the United States.

Compared to aggressive people in the middle east the similarity's are remarkable. So are the ways our government deals with domestic home grown terrorism , they do not eliminate the cause. They do not consider the cause to be the most important factor to stop the insanity of it all. If they put even 10% of the cost to stop a aggressor after the fact , into eliminating the cause they would be operating at a very substantial success rate in comparison to present policy's.

Ask any doctor if people had taken care of them selves and not induced problematic health deviation's they would not get sick , or get cancer and many disease's but then a doctor would not make lots of money , and there would not be a need to spend billions of dollars on research and cures for things that did not arise.

I had a very honest dentist when I was younger he used to always tell me to floss , and brush my teeth, and I would not have problems and you would not have to go thru painful procedures to repair them.

In order for progress to take place for any purpose their must be a proactive element maintained , and if discipline is required to uphold this it might be easier to use humility first , then to just condemn the misled people. This works there have been programs in the Los Angeles area that have developed programs that offer a alternative to gang violence , drug abuse , and non fostering of education. I have personally been involved with start ups of such programs, it works. Its also a more economical method to deal with the alternative that being police , prisons , probation officers , court process costs. It also helps to develop intelligence , for a deficit in new professionals that cannot keep up with a ever expanding population.

This breaks the cycle of poverty something I learned from my father. He had expressed to me before he died that he was preoccupied with the children in the world , I think at that time he was maybe thinking back to when he was young , and realized what was needed to be done , I am just glad that I realized what he was getting at , because it has given me a sense of purpose since he had died , that was missing in my life since then.

Intelligence is the only thing that separates us from failure. Practical , technical, its all important , information is what the world now uses to keep up with it's self. It's what a aggressor uses to achieve there goal's. Every private , commercial , governmental , ect. agency in the world is operating on the basis of collected information , intelligence , refining these type's of resource's has become easier with modern machine's , however the work has to be un-interrupted and brought forward by people that have a desire and need to do so. This has to been done at a higher intelligence level than the aggressor, or it cannot succeed.

Waiting to contemplate these policy's is not a option , the aggressor knows that this is his edge he has over us. Its our size and complexity of our system verses there's , ours is big , theirs is small and that's there advantage, they keep things simple and to the point and do not need assignment's for the most part .
Their method is group and attack however possible, utilize what is locally available, when the goal is achieved disperse, and blend in , and education is looked down onto , and that they will try to intimidate anyone in their own culture from learning unless it is for their sick and pathetic purposes.

Let me explain one thing that's very important , the aggressor utilizes psychological effect's for his success. He gives the illusion that it's all about self sacrifice , wrong it's not , it's all about convincing their adversary us of such a thing. Promoting fear is the goal and this promotes confusion , Did Osama bid Laden blow himself up no , he get's some ignorant psychopath's to do it. a That's how it's done the utilization of ignorance, that's how any

91

war has been waged by a aggressor and the outcome successful.

It's been that way for thousand's of year's. How many more time's will these self evident concept's go unrealized. There is nothing confusing going on here to me I understand them. Government system's are motivated by this system of human discourse. I am not that smart these are easy concept's to grasp. What you do about it is the trick , and I have covered it in basic theory.

Now who will execute procedure's , this is the important thing at this time. The individuals that will not except responsibility are known , they are the one's that continue to perpetuate the ongoing never ending cycle of ignorance , for their personnel gain , and acclamation of status. Here are some examples of the titles such people hold. I will not mention any names because it is irrelevant, and that it would not do any good to do so, there power comes from their status regardless of the individual that is primarily responsible, besides they might try to sue me or have me killed if I did. Believe me I know who they are it's obvious so do you.

Most all President's and or dictators of all country's. Most all their immediate subordinate's , that are a party of their regime. Most all anti party members to the above. Most all government upper level employee's of the systems that make up the executive office's of such institution's. All aggressive combatant's of the above listing, and their subordinate's.

As you can see there is pattern and a hierarchy to their way of life. It start's at the top naturally. I do not list the bottom of the chain , the soldier's that actually carry out the order's or atrocity's of the executive authority because they have been compromised , and do not have the ability to under stand what they have done , for the most part and that they did not conceive or ultimately plan or understand the long lasting results , mostly because they were uninformed , or are sick, or in need of rehabilitation , or they did not go to Harvard.

Someone once said to forgive them they no not what they do, with his final breath , he was so right. However the executives did know what they were doing and need to be held responsible ultimately, while they live ,the punishment that would continue after their death is not humanly possible for us to inflict .

This final redemption of vengeance is only possible by God , only he can inflict what we mere mortals cannot. I can only hope that God is one pissed off dude, with such people and that his mercy is not to be taken lightly. All we can hope for is that we don't piss him off the way they did. We can only speculate on how much of a bitch pay back will amount to. (Note☺) I context the above paragraph for the benefit of younger people that might think worshipping God is only for the meek , make no mistake there is nothing meek about the wrath of God.

Chapter 9 The transformation

I would like to take up a perspective in this chapter apposed to
Chapter 8 , that is a interjection of hope for the human race. I did
not become proficient at seeing all the bad and ugly that people do
to their selves and me, buy not trying to hope and have the best
intensions in what I tried to peruse in life. There is hope but you
have to look hard to see it, and stand long to gain it.

There is a transformation of the United States of America going on,
it seems that our government employees , and elected officials and
other big business organization's are failing to have anything on
their mind except what they can gain financially. It is having a
trickle effect and effecting the people that used to be against such
ideas in that those persons did care more about ideals and the power
of positive thinking.

The leaders in our financial institutions speak of a trickle effect that
will give to the mass's if the top is up held. This is pure socialism ,
there is no such thing it is impossible. This country was founded
and defended from the ground up, and any such notion of the top
being the object defies the constitutional statement We The People.

This is not good , it is starting to erode at our values and what it is
that this country is suppose to represent. If nobody has noticed this
country has become a socialist dictator-ship . This is creating a
deficit in the art's , or any other compassionate views and
lifestyles. It is effecting us in every possible way that is not
conducive , and the only thing people seem to be compelled at is
merely talking about it for those that dare.

Most do not for fear they might be looked at as malcontent's and at
risk for what people might say or see in there honest views in that

the current trend is not honesty, and just the opposite as in conforming to the popular view that consists of doing what everyone else is doing regardless of the moral / fairness or credible implications. Plain and simple there afraid of a life that is not connected to the next corrupt asshole, or counterpart in the cycle of pathetic behavior. I should further elaborate on this and acknowledge that this is a form of sociopath disorder. This is a disease that is spreading far and wide throughout the world. It is getting out of hand, and pretty soon their will be a limited amount of recognized people that have true knowledge of the word integrity, or what it stands for.

When I say recognized I am referring to anyone that is in a position of responsibility and or a government position that would have any influence and or control for the upheaval or rectification of such a problem that is basic to civil rights and or problems that have arisen due to civil rights not being recognized and or such persons suffering from a prejudicial and or constricting effect on their life due to such disorders. As incredible is that seems it is a fact, there have been numerous books and papers that have been written by professors of notable university's on this subject , however most people that speak of such things are obviously looked down on or thought of as crazy or a threat by the powerful that control the monetary fund of leading financial institutions and governments and dismiss this as a form of rhetoric by a opposing political party, or malcontent to their totalitarian view.

Well in every society scenario of upheaval there are winners and losers of the game that's played , it does not get any easier and the competition is tough. The powerful people are not going to loose that's for sure , and if you try to go against them its very difficult. So if you want to play and keep yourself respect, sanity , or health you have to be exceptionally talented , and not afraid or intimidated.

You must have a decisive plan that insures success regardless of others that you are trying to stand up against. I do not suggest you try this at home , what I mean is if you try to voice your personal views and perceptions onto your family and friends that have known you they will judge every thing you say or peruse based on their perception of you and in most cases it is very bias for several reasons, most of them personal.

If you truly want to retain your integrity and dreams, you will have to get involved with people that you have not been involved with prior to your principle endeavor that you will set out on. This is because of the effect of non bias , based on non previous expectations , or perceptions of you. This keeps everybody more honest including you, and accountability is immediately transparent.

Every parent that loves their family basically wants them to get a long, and have respect for one another , however there are different perceptions that children have compared to parents , unless one or more of the kids try's to realize the parents wishes for the sake of the parent , however it does not work often no matter how well the attempt is tried and that's because everybody has a right to their own opinion , its not the same as the others this is normal, this is what makes us all different.

The idea that people can join together at all for a purpose is a miracle in itself. This might be the main idea anyway because you have no previous knowledge of your new found friends , they might be completely different than you had any remotely preconceived perception of, and that's what makes it great , and sometimes the cooperation is much greater than you could have hoped for from friends and family.

You need to be open and receptive towards unexpected occurrence's , they will sometimes be the best things that ever happened to you. I have personally had such things happen to me many times in life when I was younger and accredit those instances for some of the best times in my life.

96

When it happens you definitely know it, its solid , there is no hypocrisy , no preconceived judgments these are the real celebrations of life. I was first made aware of these philosophies by my father , and than I started to practice the effect my self and noticed that it works for anybody that wants to try it. I suppose it is easier to grasp such concepts when you have mentors that are experienced in such things.

How ever if you keep at it you will surpass your teacher this is natural , normal , and totally understandable.

If someone worked their hole life at something and they pass it onto you , there is no lag in your capability if you understand. Once you are good at perceiving, what you do about it is the real trick. What you can do about it is your real capability. If you have been able to gain the understanding , and you are afforded the opportunity to peruse, that's your shot don't waste it thinking about this or that or what's going to happen or what some will think other wise you will never do anything and you will have wasted your opportunity, they don't grow on tree's and they are not to be taken half hearted , or neglected or for granted, and you might not get another.

However missed opportunity's can be converted sometimes to a upgraded situation. You might miss one but gain a better deal , so you have to keep your eyes open always , besides if you work hard to better your situation you deserve a better deal. Things are always changing and you should be ready to adapt, it is a key feature to getting thru life and gaining opportunity's. Just about all normal people can sit in one place and achieve eventually, but if you are able to jump on a opportunity and not hesitate you will improve your self dramatically, this I can promise is a absolute truth. The goal is idealistically to improve your mental situation while you improve your physical status.
I am referring to what is being generated in your immediate

situation , by enjoying the fruits of your labors. It is possible but you have to have the self discipline to attain your goals.

I always use to tell people that if I would have listened to the people around me say I cant do this and I should not do that ,I would have missed all the best opportunity's that life offered me. That's because it was true, and you can be sure that if someone tells you your wrong about something that is a creditable pursuit and there not willing to even try it , or realistically look at the situation ,than they are for sure the people you don't want to listen to , even if it turns out that things did not go as planed , it was not because they said so , its more like if they would have helped maybe it would have . Those people were never in the game . There are no cut and dry answers , life is not just black and white, it is full of different conditions that lend their attributes to lots of different applications.

However you must have a extroverts attitude to see things that way , people that are solely limited to introvert conditions ,will never experience such things, and I don't believe that is a guaranty of anything .

Life is suppose to be a continual process of discovery's and or pursuits that are lent to discover your realized potential for progress in how you would like things to go. We were not suppose to be a slave of any pursuit or to do nothing but compete with ourselves and others. This is not healthy it promotes corruption because there is nothing left but a endless circle of substantiation.

When something stands out that you did not plan on, that's when you know you are on the path of awareness , now don't ask why because there is no set answer except for maybe it was the idea all along, or you deserved it good or bad ,and then all of a sudden the opportunity / occurrence magically appears , it does happen I know.

When it's something good , it's the best feeling in the world , when its something bad , it scares the hell out of you , and you are so wide awake its not even funny. I have found that the effects can be controlled if you are a positive person with integrity, and the most important thing no matter what is to not panic , sometimes you only have a little time to decide your future ,this is not a comfortable situation however you do have to deal with it.

Things are getting to the point these days were there is less and less opportunities , and you must be fairly decisive to recognize your best options and or pursuits in life. It used to be if you had a good education it would carry thru to your goals , this is true in one respect because there is a higher demand for professionals in that there is a deficit of technicians , however not every one wants to be a technician that attends and graduates a university.

The trade courses that are available are not up to current standards for today's applied science's , this is due to the fact that the teachers are not there , the curriculum is not up to spec. , and the budget required to adequately achieve this is not available unless it is pertaining to private school's , and even then the standards are considered marginal.

30 years ago their were a lot of programs , their was a real respect for applied science's it was something that had to get done , and was rightfully recognized as such , from all the different academic levels and forms. These program installations have peaked and are in decline. The main reason is that their primary goals have been achieved , and that administration's have assumed that they know what is important as far as a priority rating goes. The combination has caused a undermining of required progress in such program applications required to go to the next step of education.

Administrators are suppose to manage , they were never trained for the most part to recognize development requirements to further achieve a curriculum based on applied science's , this takes well seasoned professors , with 10 to 20 years of working experience to make and develop such programs, to not recognize these facts, completely undermines what is being taught in our university's / colleges, and the effect has traveled down to the capability of corporations and or governments, that are in need of the technicians. This is why we have a energy problem and why everything is costing more and more, that's because there is less and less .

The less is because it has to be produced by someone , and that there is a largely disproportionate amount of capability that takes all things that are considered to contribute to the product completion. When you view this in conjunction to the increased population you have inflation.

The next thing that happens is that big business has to make a profit due to its increasing size of any such corporation , We use to have a lot of sub companies and corporations that made it possible for societies to grow and flourish in major cities , this is what made America great , and then some real geniuses got the Idea that a monopolistic ideal would be more profitable because it would cut costs of the main overhead , and that they could combine talent and resources to become more productive.

These company's were also given free factory's and development incentives to bring there factories to financially distressed areas. Those are all great Ideas , if you are taking about low tech manufacturing , you could go anywhere , Mexico , China , ect . but if you are taking about manufacturing Aircraft , motion picture camera equipment , and other high tech endeavors it doesn't work , those areas of industry were built from sub-company's that took generations to perfect , and be achievable in a economic sense . When a main prime contractor leaves a geographical area they are destroying the infrastructure of that industry, in relation to the economical sense of uninterrupted and accountable production to take place. This theory is being rediscovered at this time , and that the major company's are downsizing , and being forced to recognize that , effect was the best to start with.

There is a right way to expand and take advantage of economic efficiency and a wrong way I just described the wrong way. Company's / corporations are like Aircraft it is a known fact that if it is not continually maintained and or rebuilt , and or made to not be weakened by use or age it will break after so many cycles of use. When you take into consideration of the electrical system , and the older technologies of its navigation or propulsion systems , its just not economically viable to continue its use.

Well in as much as I hate to say it , the people and there capability's are not viewed as viable as the assets they manufacture unless they are , upgraded and made more up to date. You can always sell a old airplane to some small start up company, or a less mainstream user of such equipment in a foreign country ,most of them cant afford the new equipment anyway, and that's what the airlines due. However when a Aircraft company packs it up goes to who knows where , Its pretty hard to tell someone that worked in Long Beach Calif. that if they want to keep there job they will have to move to Arizona , or Georgia , or somewhere else besides where they invested their life's savings into their home and property , and family, and even if they wanted to they could not afford to . Or they are to old , or who would buy their House if nobody's buying houses , or would they buy a new house if they cant get a loan .

That works out great for Boeing or some other giant Aircraft Company , oh there is not a other its just Boeing that builds Airliners now in the U.S. , can you spell monopoly , I believe its spelled GREED.

Also Boeing cannot deliver new planes that it needs to sell for 3 to 5 years or more of back logged orders. So I guess they will have to buy them from France, the U.S. military wants to , there not waiting they say the one they build in France is better anyway. Now that's incredible folks, if I did not no better I would say some one in the U.S. is really dumb, or they want to sell airplanes made in France.

I use to be a Aircraft technician until there was not any more jobs for someone in this country that had 30 years experience at manufacturing, and maintaining aircraft, I guess there are people out there that think , of it all like sports , you know once some one turns 30 that's it , its time to change up for the young and strong talent , the only problem is it takes 20 or 30 years of someone dedicating there life to a profession to become a renown authority / expert in there field.   So much for you had your shot up until you turned 30 .

This is what they teach the kids today or something , I don't know how these people think of this stuff , but this countries going down the drain because of this way of thinking. When the military and or civil organization's have to buy Airplane's and helicopter's built in France I would have to think what's next , we already import as much as country's like Germany , Japan , China , the middle east can turn out , even technical expert's are not in this country that are the main computer tech's that Microsoft use, they are in India. All I can say is this is out of control because there is no control, what happened to the laws in this country, who is allowing these corporate giant's to do this to our country.

Our country has been financially compromised since Reagan had taken the office of the presidency , when Clinton came in the early 90's he sealed the deal and it was all down hill from that point. So you see it's not a particular party that has done this it's all of them working in competition that has brought this problem to it's current configuration. Our government is in need of a complete overhaul and rethinking of how and why it operates. The problem must be recognized and dealt with appropriately.

Chapter 10 Deficit of knowledge

When the qualification of knowledge has become limited , there is
no responsibility for anyone to understand , then it turns into a
trend , and when it becomes normal as is the case , you would think
that somebody is going to do something about it to at least insure
their own future. Upper management most of the time
are not qualified to understand what is required to uphold continuity
in performance within a company's infrastructure .   This is
because when people take a collage or trade coarse in management
the only thing they learn to do is generally manage. The fact is
someone has to know what there doing , so often a manager of lets
say a white collar background will have to require to have the
working knowledge of a blue collar worker.   This is where the
translation and the main failure occurs.

There are several methods that the manager will try to keep his job /
position. All of which is based on utilizing a blue collars true skill
this effect is a cultural aspect of business and that these type of
individuals are basing their company's performance on a type of
personal likeable qualification. I would have not believed this if I
had not personally witnessed this on several occasions, and that I
can say with certainty that this is more that a trend , it is truly
cultural.

I like to refer this to as the (executive decision) , a fitting name
wouldn't you say. Again I am not against any particular group of
people that received training to be a manager and or executive of
some kind however blue collar work is best managed and evaluated
by people of that particular culture of specialized field experience.
Its often more cost effective also, executive type people that
received their training in life are expecting more because

they think they are worth more because they say so , apposed to their actual true worth. (sorry if someone does not respect my analogy) but this is not my opinion it is a fact of the current culture / type of common occurrence in today's work place / corporate structure.

It has a lot to do with the way people are educated , cultural work aspects and the type of people that upper management prefer to have as their subordinates. This is a matter of certain kinds of persistent individuals that are asserting them selves , out of survival to sustain weather they are qualified or not to manage. They are trying to get ahead out of persistence , and that itself is a admirable / work ethic however if the manager can not evaluate / perform & coordinate it then becomes a problem.

For the lower tech jobs this is not a problem for the most part , when it involves management personnel that need 10 to 15 years min. of real experience this is not going to work.

Money is the common denominator in motivating people , with that you can get a blue collar worker to upgrade his style , however trying to go the other way is not a matter of money it has to do with their capability, unless he or she utilizes a sub management person , this is more common and a easier way to go. it also keeps everybody preoccupied with their particular expertise.

To take full advantage of this type of arrangement the best way is for the blue collar to teach the white collar the system he uses, this way you don't need a high paid manager. This would be referred to as a new school way of thinking.

In today's world everyone is on the fast track in their mind to somewhere, however that is mostly typical in this country , in smaller and or disadvantaged place's the blue collar is happy if he just gets paid after the end of the week , and he does not have to concern himself with the political or executive part of the work, besides that's not his environment.

As I discussed in chapter 9 a sub company / vendor is the way to go because its just a matter of paying someone for what they do , and not having to worry about and or having to take into consideration all the aspects of implementations, that are considered in house responsibility's.

Aircraft company's learned this out of the necessity of process's and or multiple products required for effective production. They don't build engine's , navigation equipment , electronic , and other various sub-assemblies and that this became a standard they were able to further elaborate on ,and proven to be very successful for them. One very good aspect is that they eliminate the in house responsibility for quality assurance , meaning if there own employee's fail at a procedure they eat it. If a vendor fails they don't need to except the part or process unless it was produced to acceptable inspection levels. In the case of expensive / complex items this is a big determination as to profit or loss, and or staying on schedule.

Management is a very important aspect , management engineering is a very worthwhile position for medium to large company's to be proficient at. All aspect's of the above mentioned need to be adequately evaluated, for a profitable and higher success rate to take place.

These topics are mainly discussed for a business to be successful , however a government operation / institution is also ran on the same basis. The motive is not financial , however if that institution is not ran at a cost effective level it can not sustain itself, not to mention the tax payers , and or credit establishment's responsible (Treasury Department) are operating at a deficit. This translates into a government set national interest rate and or qualification factor that is less conducive or economical , and or less programs that are available to further institutions that require government funding , emergency services , disaster relief , and so on. The trickle down effect becomes pronounced.

At this point the inflation becomes pronounced , and that Government institutions are now raising there costs to operate in the forms and process's required to operate at every level , federal , state , and local rates for taxpayers / process cost's, pertinent to operate , permit's , fee's , ect. , . Every form of commerce enterprise material , fuel , energy , electricity , transportation , its all taxed and someone has to pay for it , that someone is you and me. If the Government could operate at a level of competency that optimized its existence , everything would be more predictable, however this not likely to occur , although that being the idea , the most we could hope for is to at least have a rate that made the price affordable to the consumers that they affect in relation to the mass numbers. In that sales tax is generally set up that way , and is proportionate in that respect.   Income tax must be set up the same way if it is to be fairly proportional and in the scope of our constitution's intension.   If this balance could be kept proportional, ultimately there would be enough tax money generated by the level of any one entity being taxed for any one period of time, regardless .

The following methodology would succeed if utilized .
Example:

There are a lot of entity's of the U.S. government that should be privatized , if this happened those entity's would be earning a profit and paying income tax to the treasury instead of the treasury having to pay for their sustainment , County Hospital's , all postal system's obviously, FedEx , UPS ,DSL developed into the best most efficient postal and freight corporations in the world.   The FAA, NASA , NOAH, U.S Forestry Service, Department's of Water - Power & Gas. These are all agency's that operate at a deficit , somewhat dysfunctional , dangerous , already some what supplemented by private company's or corporations , at this time.

There are plenty of commercial company's that would qualify , to run and or invest in such company's . If only the government would stick to making and enforcing rules , everything would fall into place , including the Government's capability to operate at its optimal.

There is really not a legitimate reason why these institutions or entity's are not managed or ran privately at this time . There are presently many private corporations that are considered private contractors utilized by the Government, that are more than qualified to operate / manage the mentioned. The Governments job should be to set the price / standard's and that's it. That would make it competitive , to achieve the service company that is qualified at the best rate. That means the government should stay in the business as a manager , and let people manage business. It would be the fair way to do things ,and it force's everybody to be honest.

A system of operation , that combines government management with private management already exists. A natural progression would be to further elaborate on the privatizing of operations for consumer service's, other than the government being the only managing operator of the existing system. Safety is enforceable if operated to the same standards that the Government ran entity's are answerable to. The Government's role in the enforcement of its legal system must be more efficiently conducted. It is bogging down the country and the world for that matter. If the government contracted out and then earned a return on tax from all the subcontractors performing , it would have a surplus that could be used to run the legal system , and plan for its expansion , the requirement is only going to increase , it is stretched and under capability for required enforcement needed at this time.

Government engineering is a important procedure that needs to be considered as a continues uninterrupted / ongoing process that is continually upgraded at the optimum possible time. It should not be a politicians policy , opinion , or pursuit unless backing , data supports such planning implementations. If a non-interrupted, pursuit to render government operation's / planning is properly and continuously pursued it would not matter what political employee was in the present office position of management.

The government is a product of commercial practice's in that the same or similar policy's are exercised, good or bad are the trends that will take place. This is due to cultural trends that are popular with how society's current trend standard's are prevalent in the various rejoins. This is not a correct way for business or operation's of a business or institutions to take place , however never the less it goes on because people are a society based culture by nature. The only way society can come out of its over capacitated state is by proper planning. There must be proper safety precautions in place to protect it self. These precautionary measures must be automatically perused, constantly , this takes time and money.

Most all governments do not have the time and money at this critical point in history and if a major cultural shift does not take place to insure the continuity , stability , and integrity of a system , the whole thing will continue to unravel , it will become more severe and the frequency of the deficit occurrence's will increase.

There must be a proactive policy towards the management engineering required to accommodate society, there is not a other option otherwise it will sink from the inefficiency of its own bureaucratic mistakes. A proactive incentive must be made to be sought by the people , they need to get behind it , or it will not take.

There must be a stimulus plan that evokes participation at a cultural level. This does not come from the promise of easy money or fear it also doesn't come from the governments in respect to cultural aspect's unfortunately, non-participation in helping the average person to achieve such a change in thinking and work ethic. If the people that are supposed to be enthused by a policy are not it

109

will not attain success.

I will give the following example as to what I believe to be very relevant and necessary for such a cultural aspects to begin in the United States.

Example:

If the enforcement of laws is over enforced and or the fines for basic enforcement or policy action can not be enforced at a rate that the general public can afford, the effect gets wildly out of control , in that the enforcement procedure , is some what based on the performance of the enforcer.

The enforcer has to deliver a quota of enforcement's, this put's undue stress on the enforcer to show he or she is performing correctly . There for causing mistakes and or unfair or unrealistic conditions to apply to the general public, and there inability to comply.

If the public cannot comply with such enforcement regulation , they cannot produce , they cannot pay income tax , or property tax or any of the other taxes that the government counts on from its subject's. They also cant pay for anything else because they will get thrown in jail, because they did not come to a full stop before turning right at a intersection. Or they were going 5 or 10 MPH over the posted speed limit. It is amazing how many people end up in jail, there vehicles impounded and all the other effects down the line that start a incredibly ignorant chain of events to take place. This is a form of ethnic cleansing. I know this because it happened to me when I was younger.
I could not afford to live in Los Angeles Calif. my home town.
If this would not have happened to me , in the community where I worked and lived , and paid tax's , and contributed to the community I would not have believed it.

My father is dead now because of such ignorant policy's. he was at the time 78 years old, a WWII veteran , a key member of the civil defense system , and a upgrading participant of co-government civil participation of organizing for disaster relief personnel started in the late 1950's , a contributor and volunteer to NASA in that he participated in research projects not asking for anything in return. The company he worked with assisted the Los Angeles Police dept. in apprehending perpetrators of armed robbery's and or violent crime's .

He also assisted the FAA in gaining a understanding of certain information that local government employee's were not up to speed on, at no charge in that he felt safety is a concern that the whole community should participate in with out thinking of them selves first and or for profitable motives. He did all those things and a lot more to help develop his community , the United States and the free world in various country's. He worked and lived this life style his whole adult life.

He was cited by a LAPD motorcycle officer pulling over people at random for minor traffic violation's (ticketing task force) what a joke , in his case his front license plate had become loose , and that he decided to remove it until he returned home to install the proper hardware screws to fasten it on properly. The license plate was sitting in the back seat of the car with the hardware, I was with him and I witnessed and became a part to this and all that followed. I had asked the officer to please not site him in that the plate was in the back seat and I could re-install it.

I explained to the officer that this would cause a problem to my father in that he was to old on a limited fixed income and for health reasons ,it was not a practical reason for him to be subjected to the requirement of a follow up inspection at a LA county Sheriff

111

inspection station to show the full , technical requirement to have his license plate , re-attached with 2 screws , a 2 min. installation, I could have performed at that time in front of the officer.

I was his main care taker for the most part. On the morning of the inspection required to have his car inspected he was not feeling well and could not attend the inspection. I normally would take him with me every place. I went because he did not have anyone else that would take care of him or attend to his problems associated with his health or daily living requirements.

I made a decision to leave him at home while I made the inspection appointment for him. I had thought if I got there early it would avoid a lengthy process. For some reason the inspection had become bogged down , maybe I disrupted some ones coffee break , I don't know but I waited for a hour in a half for this big license plate inspection that only required a officer to see that it was attached and that I would be on my way. The whole ordeal had taken all morning, when I returned home I had discovered my father had suffered a substantial stroke.

I had taken him to the Hospital , after one week he died. All that because he did not have his front license plate screwed on that day. This traumatic experience effected me for years, I could not understand why as a valued member of his own community how some one could be treated with such disregard, by the same system of people that he helped and educated. I have experienced this type of occurrence 1 year after my fathers death, and that from the result of similar demonstrated ignorance of a government entity the FAA , I had been found guilty by assimilation and not any facts that would substantiate my guilt
in being neglectful , for what I was being sited for, and that in fact I had acted under the current FAA procedure that I had personally discussed with FAA personnel . I had always been truthful with them , in fact so much so it costed me my job , as a chief inspection person at a local Air charter maintenance facility, in that by me disclosing information voluntarily with out being provoked

do due so, safety related concerns of importance that would substantiate my integrity amongst other things I had been on record to be a contributor of FAA policy's. The FAA appreciated my coming forth and thanked me.

The FAA , of a different sector was investigating a crash that they concluded was absolutely pilot , error. However they needed to show that they were on the job, this had happened approx. 4 months after 9-11 / 2001. They had decided that I would make a good escape goat , or so they figured from other ideas ? me having signed a inspection process off.

I had been stripped of all my maintenance and pilot privileges , that had taken me my whole life to achieve, with the help of my father. I was able to reapply after 1 year however at that point I could not afford the reapplication process.   My health had begun to deteriate from lack of being able to earn a living , I was found by my peers as a person they should not associate with because of the FAA findings and no one would hire me based on my bad record thanks to the FAA. The same people that my father assisted in the pursuit of their career's.

 At this point due to the economy , and the current financial crisis, the opportunity / current market application was severely lowered. Because of many factors that were not corrected for due to government policy, my father and I were forced to not have a existence that was planned, like everyone else's , like there's that they made important so much so that the government destroyed ours.

These type of mistakes happen all the time , and that the innocent end up unable to defend them self's from such over powering ignorance. It all stems from a cultural corruption that is destroying our country, and the world.   I am not speaking of these things because I am upset, I am speaking because if people do not resolve

113

their differences it will become worse and to what point can only be speculated , however it does not get much worse than when innocent people die and or are falsely prosecuted, and or have become bankrupt.

The United States government is operating at a capability / knowledge deficit. It does not appear that there will be much hope for correcting this process unless a cultural awareness takes place that first acknowledges its problems and then initiates a procedure to repair the problem , and that there is a provision in policy to insure that these occurrences are not repeated by future parties and or policy. This is best achieved if a quality control / attention to policy's and procedure , integrity is maintained, and not interrupted for any reason. The complexity and burden to enforce such a procedure cannot be put on the innocent as it is now , because they are the victim and that they are unable to stand up to the powers to be that roll over them like ants.

There must be a advocate for the victims of the system to utilize with out cost to them , since the size and complexity is of the systems, and is by nature caused by the government then they must be responsible in up holding the rights of the victims. They do this in part however it is half hearted and only covers the more basic scenarios. Complete comprehension must be exercised to fairly accommodate the people that are to have enforcement policy's propounded against them.

To the extent of what I am pronouncing above applies , it is going to become unmanageable if preparation in management engineering is not taken as a serious issue that requires immediate involvement. There is a extreme amount of corruption and non-professionalism existing in the continues monitoring of systems and government operations that are safety , financial , and required future planning procedures needed for expansion or operational considerations of higher density use .

114

These are not fill in the blank position's , they require expert qualification's that take many years to develop. The wage cannot not dictate the qualification acceptance standards ,or of any compromising of personnel qualification. If the government cannot handle this responsibility they need to have it contracted, before people have their safety , and or lively hoods compromised.

The United States will go thru a cultural awareness weather they want to or not, this country is going to run on a industrial basis , because of one reason the banking institutions have been stretched out to the rest of the world. If compliance to outside country's is not complied with the institutions of those company's will be in the position of having a financial war with the U.S. this could prove to be worse than anything going on in Iraq or Afghanistan. If things continue the way they are presently 9-15-08 the government wont have to worry about a war , because it will not have the money to conduct such a thing, unless a government takes over the industrialized institutions . Once this happens a modern day version of a depression will take place. There will be complete bank insolvency except for the last one standing . The stock market will crash along with any ideas of people making money on other than industrialized trading / buying / selling .

This might not be a bad thing , it will teach the easy money people a lesson about not killing the goose that lays the golden eggs , and then every body has to start all over again. I would strongly advise that if you have any money saved , or real estate that is industrial based to hold onto that , it will be one of the few things worth anything in the future. Geographic locations will also be affected, because of the fact that industrialized ventures will have to be society based to gain a competitive and or affordable rate to be produced . It will no doubt return to the proximity of a high density environment , Major City's. that have spent the past 80 years producing product's / service's particular to industry (society) regions will have there capability once again.

115

Chapter 11 When it comes down

Many people talk about the bottom of the market hitting and then
there will be a bounce back, well don't count on that any more , you
can only bounce so many times and then there's no more bounce in
the ball. The real bottom of the market on the current housing crisis
will not be fully realized for 2 more years, buy that time there won't
be much left of the current banking institution's , this will drive the
interest rates , and qualification aspects to higher amount's and
qualification standard's.   Current real estate will have to be
liquidated by law , very cheaply for those that have the money
(cash) source's,   this will further lower the value of the property
because there is so much available.

The amount it costs to purchase will be raised in disproportionate
area's.   The less of a desired area the more the banks will not be
able to liquidate the surplus properties. , a nd the less motivation for
 buyers to purchase in the less selective areas.

This leads to the reversal of all the aspects that led to the current
crisis, that's because impulsiveness led to the crisis.   When
problems are developed by this impulsive buying and selling of
property / money market's , than everyone becomes frightened and
the hording and ultra conservative reactions take place. This further
complicates and cause's a even more pronounced slump , the other
side of the problem comes from the ultra rich , competing with them
selves to find a easy tax shelter / investment system. It had become
very easy for the big bank people to gain foot holds in area's that
resulted in the disruption of equilibrium required to balance the
working class and the work , vs. a surplus that had built up from the
upheaval of it all. There have been programs in the past that
regulated the amount of a price hike that would be allowed, in

certain city's that amounted to rent control.

There must be controlling safety financial factors that are in place to control the escalation and or reduction of a population vs. pay scale so as to not cause the uncontrollable runaway financial upheaval seen in 2008. When there is nobody watching the effect's and controlling the balance of a situation it spell's trouble for everyone, regardless of your political status or belief's. You could be 100% coorect in saying deregulation has caused this current situation there is no other greater factor that occurred.

The amount of trends and causes that contributed to the problems of the bank failures are not complicated although very selectively , configured to have lots of secondary business's feel the effect , this is completion that leaves the controlled as its victims. Just about any type of solid asset industry can have a glut of equipment on the market , and that it might suffer a little. There is no industry like the banking / monetary fund management.

The banking industry funds all the rest of the industries, it is impossible to not affect the banking industry if the spending characteristic of society are variable. However the industry spending / credit given with out collateral is what the banking industry is based on, that means its based on trust that you can pay, for its services.

If the banking industries cannot develop creditable clients it should not loan money that is federally insured , its not legal , there are guidelines established that are federal laws, that make the loan officer responsible to not arbitrarily loan money that's federally insured, to unqualified individual's .

If the federal government suggests that guidelines are followed , that's because they know from years of experience that such guidelines have the best case scenario for success.

The loans that have been given out the past 6 to 8 years had no solid asset's of collateral to base them on. They did not have a verified income , nor did the real estate brokers / loan officers care because every body got a credit rating. If you had no credit you just became a lower score and the loan only costs you more, or the terms were not great or , there would be some way the loan officer could close the deal. The Idea that a loan officer or a realtor would not have to go thru proper evaluating and reviewing buy federal employees is a gross mistrust on the governments part for allowing such actions to take place.

When it comes to money everybody is good ? where did some body get such a idea, and who let people say and exercise business practices this way, with federally insured money. How do banks get away with risking other people's federally insured money, The Treasury Department seems to be having a problem keeping an I on who is exercising business practices with the fed's money, intelligently. Well even if the fed says this is there problem and they will deal with it. How? , What about all the foreign country's that are going to sue the U.S. government because their money is no longer where they put it , and that they will form a class action suite to combine all their debt. concluding to gross mismanagement of other country's investments into the U.S.

If this was 60 to 80 years ago I wonder if it could have been responsible for starting WWI, and WWII , because it sure does fit the pre era banking practices , where gross miss management of international trade and ventures that left some people a little upset about a few things, that went on in certain European country's.

Due to the global economy there will most likely never be a WWIII because it would mean total world annihilation , but in as well it would mean that the opposing nation would loose its interest in the country they invested in un less it was a country by design that

119

would facilitate certain features of world trade that could be claimed and or consumed for dept. or other reason's., there for people are going to get back at people financially, it is the battle ground of the 21st. century, and that the innocent will pay , with the ignorant , the only people that can survive or thrive are not necessarily bad people (as far as investors that did not engage in the ignorance or lack of ethical banking practice.) , however they must be as wise as the situation they will enter into , and beware of every thing or person that could compromise goals , the trick is to achieve this knowledge and try to achieve your sense of control from the entire experience, when everything around you is spinning wildly out of control at time's, now if it were easy for everybody there would not be Trillions of dollars in debt incurred, by the United States, or its all just a ploy that has lent it self to cause massive debt.

It is a combination of many factors, however the blame must be someone that you can put your trust into. However it's not that easy seeing how the entire world markets are effected, there is no doubt that the United States has been used by domestic and foreign entities that have been apprehensive to the neglect for regulation that we suffer from here in the U.S. and what we will allow anyone to have , for the most part, there way. This is just as much the fault of the Banking organizations that let greed override common sense as anyone else that acted senselessly. On this day 9-17-08 it finally hit me as to the seriousness of the worlds wasted financial loss's that were all thrown onto the worlds biggest scam , that there ever was, and it all came from the United States.

It seems that the world was determined to blame the U.S. on being the worlds trouble maker, well it seems now they really have something to be pissed about, and that there is no question that it is the fault of the United States , as to who is responsible for having a insolvent democracy , some might call the U.S. a Hypocrisy , these people would say such things to make them selves feel better , or want to blame someone, but they participated in the hypocrisy so they cant say to much , infact anyone that invested in such

120

hypocrisy , were part of the problem . What problem ?
well the problem of not reinvesting in the same way you earned
your profit's.

You can't just suck ever thing dry and expect the source that was
causing the profit being generated to just feed them self's like
house's out on the range. I meant horse's. Let me put it this way
if you beat the slaves , and don't feed them or give them water and
they die who's going to do the work?

That's what happens if the money that was made thru the use of the
masses is not reinvested into the system of the masses it cant
sustain, the masses grow but the requirement to sustain them is
manipulated by greedy people not worried about it later on down
the line , and or what the result. is People are the machine that need
oil , gas , maintenance , if they don't have what they need to live
they can't make the rich people money its just that simple, in fact if
they were given a fair deal, the rich people would even get richer,
but greed is no good , it kills , it does not build thriving society's .

It is a total lack of knowledge and will stop the richest , most perfect
scenario there ever was for people that went to collage to learn
about investing to become complete failures. So if your one of the
people that works for one of those failed company's you are most
likely seeking to park your resume somewhere else, most likely
another industry , there are probably a lot of unemployed banking
loan officer's these days.

The Biggest survive because if they fail they drag the whole system
down, there for they get to do what ever they want because their
running the show. They get to buy up who didn't make it, there is
a lot less competition when the dust settles. The small ones go the
way of the week species , or the injured and or maimed they are
sure prey for the strong over powering beast to conquer .
Thinning of the herd , only the strong survive. In as much as I
might describe what goes on , and compare it to animalistic

121

behavior that's because it is, animalistic. No matter how nice those old gentlemen look and sound on television , they are saying exactly what they want you to here and it sounds good to , that's because they have been manipulating money there whole lives , 50 , 60 year's , they were born into it , their parent's were good at it , and there parent's parent's, were good to, so just think about it , they must be pretty dam smart, and if some of them don't look cool that's because it's part of the image.

Make no mistake there are winner's and loser's , and if your keeping score like I am, get to learn all about this trading / company profile characteristic's. It's quite a game these people play. It really is on monumental level's , I guess the whole trick is to learn a new trick , how to make a faster buck. Or how to get someone else's, I guess that's easier from what I can tell, So what does integrity or ethic's have to do with making money , nothing but if you don't want to run out of money while your playing monopoly , you have 2 choices , get more monopoly money or the players have to loan the bank money, apparently the world is at that point.

OK it's the extended play championship, so who ever win's this one get's a lot of money when the dust settles. Well it looks like its getting late we better continue the never ending game tomorrow.

That's the nature of it all it never stops , it never will, if it does WWIII start's. Since it all comes from the U.S. than they can print as much money as they want and make the whole world rich if they want , because they are the bank # 1. What could someone dispute if the money comes from the treasury dept. it's U.S. legal printed currency. Come to think about it the world ouw's the U.S. Treasury dept. , I think it's perfectly acceptable to print more money , however it should at least get aimed at the people that were ripped off by the greed of the system, that would be fair enough, but since the true origin of the core greed is rooted in the head of

122

government's this will most likely never happen in a million year's, or maybe if Jesus Christ came floating down to earth , declared that he felt he needed to speak about pay back, and how it might not be looked at by him favorably if the correct restitution's were not made. Short of that I don't see anyone's government on this planet acting responsibly and or fairly , concerning such thing's. I don't see how they could, it was a drastic disrespect for integrity of how the world operated that drove the situation , it is something that has been going on constantly for about 20 year's at its present pace.

This is as rooted to greed as it possibly could get , and that the breaking point has occurred. How to fix that which had taken 20 years and a .com culture to evolve , and then suddenly change that situation with any amount of money. They will throw billions of dollars at them self's to try and put a giant band-aid on the problem. It's not going to work everybody is going to loose . The government is trying to save face and or their crappie jobs in light of this horrendous ordeal, of neglect and complete disrespect for the so-called lower cultures, the blue collar worker's are the only ones that will be standing when everything is said and done.

The jobs / investment's that employ technician's , mechanic's , machinist's , manufacture's , farmer's and all the rest of the hard working profession's will be the new power wielder's, and the true responsible individual's that really make or break the economy. There is going to be so many laws passed , that will rectify investment policy's , that it will become very selective , and lend it self to only the most powerful , or educated analyzer's to be able to compete in a very competitive market.

There will be a real basis for the loaning of money , and that someone's word, that theyknow what's going to happen will be just a memory of the past , because the world has been tapped out because of ignorance , and true knowledge that was ignored.

It would be accurate to say that deregulation is what triggered this to happen, this is how it started (Ronald Reagan) he had the best intentions but failed to realize that there would be people that were extremely smart at money manipulation, more so than anyone had any idea. It was facilitated with the use of computer's and digital instant response equipment . Than not to be out done the Clinton administration opened the flood gate's. and facilitated the ability for un-restricted de-regulation. At the end of that ,the Bush administration went whole hog, and more or less stated this will be the mother of all government influenced spending that will be driven to the core , and that the most faithful and closest to the administration will get their earned reward for being loyal party patriot's.

So you see it's not what you call your self , more than what you do to define your status, and there is no doubt on who has been defining there self , the greed factor has been operating at 100% for some time now and that it can no longer proceed as it has been , and that it's all come to a head on this month of September in 2008, the month that the financial world fell on it's face, and that there is no amount of plastic credit card surgery that will restore it's beauty that it once had. It's like that old Hollywood actress that had to many cosmetic surgery's and that she's permanently scared from it now.

There is a good reason why China & India run the world now, they invested in it with hard work , and we taught them , educated them , helped them , thinking we would benefit , being the great middle man that we are here in the U.S., only problem is that the student has surpassed the master, and nobody banked on that. They did not figure there were people out there starved to make money , and all they needed was the advent of the digital age, and that was it. They built these computer's in all the suppressed country's by the million's and that the price got down to nothing. The government's of these suppressed country's learned that this was the future , and they acted. Remember during the Viet Nam era how the best stereo's were obtained for very low price's if you were stationed in Korea I do. A lot of people that in listed told me that this was the best thing, next to all the cheap drugs you could buy. This included Afghanistan , Libya , and many middle eastern countries. Yes those countries were at in the seventies. It was our government that got us there and there wasn't even a war at the time.

Chapter   12   Who is going to pay

That is the Trillion dollar question who ? , Everybody, most of all
those that have the least, and are considered the least important buy
the one's that have the most. It could not happen any other way.
There is no more middle class America as of Sept. 2008 . Just the
rich and the poor , no more in between. The in-between lost their
job , their 401K , there investment portfolio, there house , there
big car, there extravagant life style that everybody said was OK to
peruse because all their friend's were , and it was the current trend,
and it's all good , well I guess it wasn't that good.

Their will now be a cultural revolution and it will be un-stoppable
due to the current situation. This revolution will come from those
that have been left with nothing or next to nothing , and decided
they have to pick up the pieces, like it or not its just not going to be
the same, and they have to do what has to be done to survive. This
will lead to many numerous scenario's . Local government's will
react and due the only thing they due, start blaming someone.   It is
normally the victims, they will have all sorts of problems , like
drug and alcohol abuse , people going to jail , crime , more home's
and apartment's being vacant, a very large dis-proportionate amount
of have's compared to the have not's will occur.

The people with money will continue to have there way , and things
will not get better until the have-not's take their life's into their own
responsibility and stop relying on the people with money to help
them they will not.   As far as the government they will be in a
battle with those trying to tread thru all of this, including member's
from their own competitive environment, that are only there for the
money , and that's the bigger percentage of them.   The world has
turned into a very unpredictable place , there is no doubt, so why
doesn't the Government's of the world get it , apparently the bank's

are trying to help their crippled world survive. For some reason the government thinks they are above the monetary system because they print money. They need to be able to pass laws that say it's OK to print money how many time's do they think they can get away with it before people start to say where's mine , or who said you could do that . We have laws that specify their must be a plan or it's just socialism. That's why we kicked England out and we had our revolution / constitution party / battle's. All those people died so the privileged get more money and the poor that worked , and had to fight to uphold the rich get nothing in the end, that's not democracy , it's just a mockery.

It's time that people with a plan did something , and it has to come from the people that need it, they are the victim's of this mockery of democracy. Instead of the government giving billion's of dollars to bank's that don't need the money why don't they give the surplus housing to people that need it , it would fix a lot of problems. There are plenty of displaced FEMA victims of natural disaster's. There are a lot of people that would not be homeless if they had a place to live there are sick and elderly that do not have a place to live, there would be more hopeful causes, instead of the everlasting hopelessness that is continually pounded into those that have nothing .

It's time to give back to the people that built this country.
How could our so-called leader's do this you ask, well it's very simple they led and other's followed. It's the nature of the game , you know follow the leader, they taught us that in elementary school remember, than in high school , than collage ,
then the military , the corporate structure, ect , ect.   The government has a motto they must have invented because they have been exercising it for a long time. " You cant fix it if it's not broken" It's not we better fix it , because it's going to break, or it's to dangerous if we don't fix it , I have personally witnessed this policy being exercised thousand's of time's. I hate to say it but our government is a whore, and she will suck-up to who

ever is the best sugar daddy that she can get.

I did not say the United States is one, I love my country and so did many people that are dead now , and there memory deserver's better than what a bunch of political / financial domestic terrorist's are doing.

They have no right to do what they were allowed to , and get away with it for the past 20 year's. There is no disguising that de-regulation / non-supervision is responsible. I know I watched the whole thing as I was torn down by friend's , and family because they thought they were entitled. When thing's did not work the way they wanted, they had to blame somebody , hey I know how about blame the guy that warned us all this would happen, yeah he must be a witch or something, he's always talking about trouble , and he does not see the positive side to thing's , and the bad thing's happen like he said , yeah it must be his fault. They did that with Jimmy Carter.

When I was younger and studying to be a pilot , I was taught by many different instructor's most of them pretty good. They all had one thing in common in what they taught , and that was this . If you wait too long to make a decision while your in the air , you only have so much time to react or contemplate the situation, and then it's to late your dead. I was always looking for other planes out there , or where am I going to land if my engine quit's, or where is a obstacle , or will I have enough gas , or should I completely trust a air traffic controller 100% , was maintenance properly performed. I would have died dozens of time's for those reason's arising when I least expected it.

If I was not aware that it could only take one thing to go the wrong way , and it would just ruin my whole life, it would have happened many times, way to many in that the reason I am not dead is because I was aware of the possibility of a problem occurrence, that did occur , and that I was able to react and control the situation, before it became completely out of control.

128

I did not have the choice of ignoring what was going on around me ,
I had to act responsibly or there would have been extremely
negative consequence's. This work ethic translated into my daily
life , and that I could count on being able to sleep better at night
because of it, however I did suffer financially / personally.

In most case's the people at the top of the financial ladder were not
concerned with such thing's and or other indirect participant's in
what was required to achieve a safe and responsible consideration
for situation's that required attention to be paid to detail's.   This
attitude towards requirement's for proper business dealing's has led
to all the present day problem's that are taking place all over the
world. For the most part it comes from people not following thru
with what and who it is that should be recognized for insuring
proper consideration's.

Sudden desperate Government bail outs are nothing short of special
interest socialism that will only help the presently guilty. The
bankruptcy law is far more fair in helping or protecting banking
institution's that have gone too far with out being regulated.
Those institutions are not going to wait for the government once the
ship is known to be on its way down , they will get off , cut their
loss's , and move on or join the group that is surviving, and or have
a idea what to do next.

They can only wait so long for the government to initiate their
safety net , and most of the time it is a failure and that people that
counted on help because the government said they would act , are
left discouraged because they did not act and or it was not the
preferred or promised expectation.

The next thing that happens is the survivors and or stronger ones,
will take advantage of their surroundings and use the whole thing to
make even more money, this is perpetual.
What would happen if the rest of the world was so liberal , or the

129

rest of the laws ?. There would be people getting away with murder left and right , just because they said they were sorry , these are the same people that are considered the religious right. They believe they can do what ever they want as long as they say there sorry before they die , and that they want Jesus to come to their salvation so that they can walk in his ways , after a life time of sin? What kind of religion is that , well it's the one that says you only need to act with your mouth , and everything is good.

The same one our current administration uses to substantiate their policy's. I always thought we were not suppose to inter mix church and state. I don't remember anything in the bible that said , the government had any authority that was joined with god. However it does say that pay on to God what he wishes , your true honest hart, and that what ever you incur with government is between yourself and the government, in that the government is only a instrument of keeping order within a group of people, a society of people that does not operate on any other basis besides total equality, the main reason being that at the time of Jesus , there were so many different forms of excepted or denigned religions and that they all only developed into corruption, including his (not of his doing).

The point is Government rule is society organized for profit to all those that participate, that it self does not make it bad or evil however it does not say that it is automatically good , the origin of the United States had proven that when it became intolerable for United States to continue under British rule.

The Ideals and philosophies of the originals formed from Brittan were of a noble and honorable one , however they are only instrument's subjected to use , and are only as honorable or dishonorable depending on their uses. The same goes for the U.S. , Russia , South America or any other society in the world, no one is above God. How could they be God is God , even the bible states so apostles or no apostles, there is only one God and he says who he is and no other , and he did , the Judea , Christen , Moslem , ect. they all ultimately state that God declares that he is who he is , and there will be no debating or compromising of that explanation regardless of how wise any human being thinks he is.

So the sooner people get over the fact that their not God's , because they have money the sooner they will be living in reality. There have been many recorded case's in history where people that were born with nothing , but their health if they were so lucky , went on to become very successful noteworthy people, and even more so because they were not born into money and that they had to strive and work very hard to be accomplished. If anyone is closer to God than the other of us on this planet , than they must be defined by their action's. God definitely was he did not just talk a good deal he delivered, humbly closed it better than any one else , and set it straight up in everybody's face , like it or not.

I really enjoy making comparisons on the hypocrites compared to the humble people , that are the real salt of this earth. They always were , always will be, if only the greedy , and controlling money giant's could aim their frustrated financial ambitions in the right direction , they would be happier , they would feel better about them self's , they might even get a idea of what its like to have had a real life, most importantly they could say they helped to stop a fellow human being's suffering , and did something to contribute to the human race.

So far the big money people have only demonstrated just the opposite. It really is a pathetic display of so much money that came from greed , that was turned into so much worthless waist , its likening of a biblical proportion , prophesized even, and not to mention that the whole world is affected, hey maybe this is it, financial Armageddon , the true evil I guess it would be if money was your life. I read they were jumping out of building's in the 30's when the great depression hit. I guess they only jump out of buildings now when our government lets terrorists board FAA approved airline operations. It seems to be very profitable for some banks to buy and sell them self's to each other when the going gets tough , as if the whole world was going to buy in to their lame plan / shell game.

I guess they counted on all the poor people not to be able to say anything about what is going on. Well even poor people with out a great deal of education can watch TV and the radio , and the computer ,and analyze on the side line the game scenario.

In the early 1980's most major US airlines were owned by all the same stock holders , and that the 51% owners of them were a handful of people as in maybe 10 so if one carrier was determined to be a maintenance capability for the group , it would perform all the required to keep the others flying utilizing , engines , wheels , electronic gear , ect. in that this maintenance carrier as we shall name for example:

Continental airlines because they really did this. Continental would shift aircraft, that were in need of extensive work or that they were , not worth their note payment , and became a right off for the carriers. They were then transferred to the continental fleet.

Continental would take all the junk and essentially , kept it off the competing market driving the price up for the other carriers to charge for tickets . By the way because of deregulation this was legal. To make a long story shorter Continental filed Bankruptcy and that they had millions of dollars worth of toxic debt. The other carriers profited with good working equipment (same basic stock holder's), and higher ticket prices , and a write off for icing on the cake.   Then the Bank of New York bought the Aircraft from the government at 5 cent's on the dollar , and put them into service striking up the Continental airline in operation , after the aircraft sat for 1 year. They were not at all in a legal safe airworthy condition, how ever the FAA allowed them to be flown with out noticing many of the discrepancy's that would have made them un-airworthy. This is a whole separate story that is a incredible history on how money , banks, power , and greed control destiny literally, and that anyone that had such an idea such as safety first , before money did not stand a chance in this area. By the way a South American national was the brains of all this as well as the 51% stock holder for approx. 15 of the U.S. leading airlines and as well Continental that orchestrated all this. I am sure all his wealth was deposited into a off shore or other low tax country account and its perfectly legal.

I personally witnessed management over look, such aircraft that I worked on for a maintenance company that hired me as a safty technician and avionics' maintenance tech. and that the management told me to stop finding safety issues or finding discrepancies with the Aircraft because it was becoming financially undesirable. I was soon terminated from employment because I did not feel that safety was less important than money. More so I felt that management did not want the contractor to be unsatisfied.

This type of scenario was later repeated when I was in a high management position as a chief inspector for a corporate based maintenance facility that had many Aircraft that were owned and operated by leading U.S. banks. I was also terminated for cooperating with the applicable laws required for FAA adherence. A few months later I was stripped of all my Pilot & Maintenance licensing that I worked for my whole life honestly, in that there was a post 9/11 period of policing that was being enforced by the FAA it was necessary to find fault with people in that the same way a police officer is told they need to up hold a quota of citations to show that the rules of the road were being enforced. Regardless of how I defended my self , and that I was also a quality assurance manager for a company that was supplying much needed equipment for military personnel engaged in the conflict in Iraq, I was found

133

by the FAA to be a non satisfactory example of a FAA approved
safety inspector. However that was just the opposite finding by
the U.S. war dept that found my system of inspection to not only be
creditable but vital to national security at a time of great importance
when such a thing was required for equipment utilized by U.S.
armed forces, in respect to military aircraft , NAVY , and U.S.
ground forces.   So as you can see no good deed go's unpunished.

If this gives you an Idea of how screwed up this country is , that's
just 1 personnel example I have herd and seen hundreds, of similar
situations. I told of my story to different people and had gotten
different opinions. The best explanation that I herd was from one
person that said I must have done something bad in my past life to
have such bad karma, and that if I went to the church of scientology
they could go back in to my many past life's and clear my karma. I
kept from laughing because that was just about the most ridicules
thing I had ever herd of , so I asked that person a very specific
question.

I asked him if that's really the case and I was so bad in my past life
to warrant such discipline onto me by God , than the people that
were doing what they were doing to me were either sent by God to
discipline me or that they were much worse than me , and if the
latter was the case who was going to discipline them. He could not
answer me with any explanation except that only God knows the
answer to that. I than asked him how do you know that , did God
talk to you and say this ? , did the president of the United
States tell you that , which one of the so called blessed people
informed you of Gods will, because they must be the wisest of all
people and I must have enlightenment from them,
wont you tell me , I would really like to know so I can stop failing.

Well he never was able to answer my question , maybe I was being
to specific, however he was the one that told me God was doing all
this , and that this is what he believed. I had come to my own
conclusion and that he was right it was God that was responsible

for all the bad materialistic misfortune I was having, however the God that was in my opinion responsible was not the nice , and forgiving one from above , it was of the one that rules the earth , and it is the one from below that was cast down , as the story goes.

In the human race is society based , most people do not, or understand how to separate themselves from the current trend's or groups that are prevalent , and mainstream . That is because for the most part they fear the unknown, of not knowing for sure what the outcome will be or how their future will prevail without a guaranty. What they fail to understand is that if they don't try an alternative they are guaranteed to not cause anything different to take place, except for further and greater despair / failure. It is impossible to further or make modification to situations if there is no desire for such things to take place regardless of what is popular or determined current standards.

The U.S. has adapted a pathetic standard practice , in that if you don't join in with the covering of the corruptible ass's you are a outcast , and will be left out of the loop. This is a effect that hits all the different forms of society and their financial levels , true evil is a non-prejudice entity it does not care about ethnicity or financial status or levels of achievement , all are welcome in this realm.

From the President to the contractor , the civil servant , the soldier , the business man or woman , all are welcome and all have participated. This develops upward to an abuse of power , civil rights , laws , every form of a society's construction has been effectedin every country of the world. This is nothing new it has been going on for thousands of years. People are amazed by this because they cant understand how this would be able to take place in the current time of technology and materialistic improvement. Corruption and or evil has nothing to do with the accomplishments of smart people there are plenty of smart evil people, and they achieve their worst effects on man kind with the aid of modern devices. This seems to be the root of confusion for most people.

135

Chapter 13   The Responsibility

Some one is responsible for the upheaval of what's going on in
societies today. There are hundreds of thousands of people that are
responsible for the atrocities being committed onto millions of
people . The problem of compromised integrity has reached
a staggering level. There is no reversing the damage, however it is
the law and moral responsibility of the people that inhabit this
planet to uphold the system of checks and balances that are
required, and that as the population grows there will be a even
more pronounced need to do so.

There are laws against abuse of power , abuse of natural resources ,
neglect of ownership responsibility. However for the most part the
extent of who or what is considered for disciplinary action , or how
long it should be in a sense of time before certain offenses are
considered no longer prosecutable. There is a theology that
is following a trend in society to lend the discipline required to be
limited to someone's opinion as to its importance.

Fair enough than why is it that our laws and the constitution itself
has been continually modified. Well the answer is because it had
been noticed that it is required. If anyone has not noticed many of
our laws giving leniency for non responsibility need be modified
because it has been noticed that smart and educated people are
taking advantage of those laws , and that there needs to be a
provision in place to not further allow such a thing to go on , not
just for the banking and money institutions, but for all parts of
society especially when health and safety are considered a
paramount factor.

I would personally go so far as to say that the people that are in
charge of our laws are responsible to make these changes as they

are required with out it taking to long and before its to late. There is
a structure for such things there called emergency revocation of a
professionally licensed person acting in a environment that has to
do with public safety. How ever the process is way to slow
when it comes to the powerful that are in power , it could take
decades because there is no advocate for the innocent until its to late
or someone is dead due to neglect of proper inspections and
controlling duties. Attenuating to public requirements needs to be
accelerated because populations and or problems associated with
mass amounts of people are more pronounced , and that it is not
going to get any easier as time goes on.

The general way that safety issue's are dealt with are always after
someone or a group of people have been killed. If this was due to
areas of uncharted experience it could be looked at as unfortunate
but not foreseeable , however there is not much these days that is
unforeseeable , and that the government and big business is using
every excuse they possible can to state that they did not know , or it
could not have been prevented, and so on. They get away with it
because there is no regulation in place that takes the unforeseen into
account.   Our legal system is complex and there are many technical
reasons for everything that is deliberated on, the idea that
unforeseeable or causes related to safety concerns are not in place is
just ridicules.

It's a matter of common sense and that the people that are suppose
to be responsible are not concerned and or too lazy to do their
respective duty correctly, and or they don't want to.

Most of the laws on the books presently are 40 , 50 , or more years
old and outdated, and are not taken into consideration , of real time
situation's that are in place globally. The world has centered itself
financially around the United States mostly because we have the
resources to accommodate everyone , and that it suites there
purposes , including domestic investors that are represented as a
entity outside the United States, like off shore banks and investment

company's.

This is completely legal , and that as long as there is a country and or place of origin to call it home this will go on , and it should because it has for a very long time. The problem is when such workings are used in a way that undermines fair practice and banking laws that are in place, and that there is anti integrity persons that are aware of all the loop holes and laws that are taking place, and or how to manipulate the governments and congress's of country's.

No one is willing to be the odd man out in this country or any other it is the way of the world and it stinks , and it is choking all the working class people that are forced to pay for it with being taxed and not represented fairly in society because of such forces. There must be a way of protecting ourselves from ourselves concerning such practices. I have personally witnessed this effect go on and that I am a victim of such, and because of laws that protect the guilty I am powerless to have any legal recourse , actually most of the injustice I write about in this book has actually taken place in my life for the past 30 years .

You might say how is it that I would let it keep happening , well it was unforeseeable and that the people I trusted and counted on did not turn out to have my best interest in their hart unless it suited their purposes. The work I have been involved with was based on if they paid me for services rendered and or , projected joint outcomes that were internationally based (U.S. / Mexico) & domestically, in respect to being contracted by U.S. company's acting in the U.S. It would be fair to say that even when I was legally allowed to peruse non payment for services rendered in Mexico , the lawyers I contracted to represent me had to be hired in a non local area to where I was engaged in business , this is because when I hired local lawyers they cut side deals with the opposition , in that the towns were small in that the lawyers I hired might or had been friends with the opposition or not willing to stand up for me to make a fair representation. I had spent thousands of dollars on attorneys fees for nothing, because it would have been considered a insult to represent a American for such purposes , and that they felt it there duty to relieve me of my money and provide non-comprehensive or false services. This is what goes on inside of Mexico and that there is no way for anyone to be represented in such a country except for certain cases ,where high fees were paid and a out of town origin attorney was utilized. This I have personally experienced , when I went to the American consulate I was told they could not help me and that advise was all they could supply. I did collect once with the help from a attorney that was from Mexico City in that he did not know any of the opposition and was not loyal to the local business men.

I have lost hundreds of thousands of dollars because of such a thing. The United States will not enforce and or protect me , and had told me I was on my own.

This had transpired just after the NAFTA free trade agreement was enacted by President Bill Clinton in that he considered himself successful in establishing , however in reality it was George Bush Sr. that started it, there for total responsibility could not make President Clinton liable. There was the dot com bubble and Bush and Clinton were taking credit for it. There were many cases and causes of distress that were involved with such tactics of the last administration starting something where the present administration picked it up, like the bungling of the first Iraq War , 911 , it was all because of the excuse that the last administration started it and it was not there fault as to why things had taken place the way they did.

This is not acceptable this abuse of power negligence must stop there will not be no way of evolving from such occurrences in international policy, and or domestic injustice. It has been almost 20 years since NAFTA was enacted and the Mexican government has still not relaxed the importation tax on its people while we have allowed their products to come into the U.S. untaxed.   This is contributing to all sorts of illegal trade and the Mexican people fleeing their country because their government has made it impossible for them to sustain above a poverty level for the most part. Why do you think 10 million Mexicans are living in the U.S. and they just keep coming , its because big business in this and there country is forcing it onto them.

They have a beautiful country , people travel from all over the world to go there on vacation , tourism is one of their highest paying economic industries. They do not flee because they don't like it there , its just the opposite , they are forced into this by the powers in there country and our country , its all just a game to big business. Its not just Mexico, this is taking place globally.

The world flees their war torn or poverty ridden countries to come here , because of the lack of enforceable civil and or business practices. If the U.S. spent a fraction of what it does on war , to implement co- existing business agreements with such countries all this could be avoided for the most part , but greed is put into play at a administrative level and nothing done spells money for those that are in power.

These are not practices that are hard to understand , they go on , and on , year after year. I'll give you a example: If the road gets washed out in some where Arizona there is going to be money from the government that's goes to a contractor to divert the run off from the hills. The contractor is on a lets do lunch with who ever makes the award of the contract , theirs a kick back , a commission paid to the government award granter.

Now that everybody's one happy family , its found that its going to take more time and money to fix the hill. By the time the hill is almost fixed it rains again , the contract is awarded for one more year, there is more money appropriated and of coarse more commission paid by the contractor to the government worker. Now imagine this , if the governments in the world had enough CIA

, FBI , police, and federal or local integrity enforcement personnel , which they don't to conduct the amount of sting operations required to enforce proper working ethics , and they were enforced there would not be anybody running the operations required for the worlds governments to function on a daily basis. It would all come to a grinding halt , and I am not kidding.

Hers another one except it really going on as I speak. Mexicans come here and work hard get paid to make babies , and support their families , than save up and make enough money , go back to Mexico and live a really good life with plenty of money and property that is acquired at a fraction of the cost that it would cost 50 miles north of where they make there investment in there home country.

This is just the legal way its done with out reverting or taking up gang or drug smuggling activities.

You can be assured that the complexity of this situation and the magnitude is staggering Not to mention the vast amount of similar devises I have described for making money that leaves the U.S.. There is a president set by the administration , that makes everyone buy into this or they will be outcast and have no job. This has developed into a system where it is considered normal , just like in Russia , and or any other small or large power of government. It is similar to a non violent mafia , however once things get to a high dollar amount it is the same as a violent mafia because people start going to jail , and or turn up dead mysteriously. The complexities of what I am taking about have penetrated to the very core of this country or any other and it applies to many parts of the government associated alliances , particularly when it comes to the military contractors , they are the worst offenders because they are profiting from brave soldiers dieing .
The military contractors make the most money from such ideals and are influencing a congress, that has been bought and paid for. Did you ever wonder why it takes 10 billion dollars a month to combat

141

a bunch of AK47 wielding heroin addicts , or why they cant be stopped. What would happen if we were in a real war with a real threat from a intelligent adversary like Russia , Germany or Japan I guess we would be as good as dead , in 5 years we could not stop a few packs of idiots with Toyota pick up trucks and AK47's with their bandito style tactics , give me a break.

I call this Texas technology because, well it comes from Texas folks I've witnessed the President of the United States say it , (quote) you don't have to be in Washington to get work done it can be accomplished with telephones and fax machines from Texas at the ranch you'll see (un-quote). Yeah well I see pretty good and I have 20/20 vision , I have seen real well the kind of work that was accomplished. In Oklahoma at the FAA headquarters located in Oklahoma City , (the show me state) they must not have windows in the FAA building because they did not see what was going on in the real world of Aviation , in that all the safety discrepancies , concerning the threat of terrorists allowed to receive training to fly Airplanes, were allowed to board planes and slit the throats of the pilots and kill everybody, and take down our country.

I hope they get better contractors some day that will build buildings with some windows so those people at the FAA in Oklahoma can be shown what's happening in this country , I understand that they must be shown (the show me state), however I figured that its pretty obvious , they cant be shown because they cant see out of the building they work in , am I missing something ? Oh excuse me for being sarcastic, but would someone explain it to the friends and family members of the victims from 911 and or the 911 commission report that says their was a definite failure in the governments responsibility to have foreseen such things being probable. Oh your sorry , well maybe if the people that spent as much time worshiping God were as dedicated to the fact that the Devil is the other end of the story here on earth, they might be a little more prepared , would someone install some windows in that building please.   Where did it ever say in any bible teachings that the meek will inherit the earth by being meek minded , I never read that. Where did it say that the United States was defended by merely petitioning the lord with prayer. What about all the brave ever loving souls that sacrificed their life in battle for their country , and in Jesus name. They certainly were not meek minded, or spirited , they fought with conviction , and only asked if they would be remembered at judgment day by our maker. Well I am not from Oklahoma but I have been shown what the government in this country thinks of our brave dead brothers and sisters.

Every time I think about the way this administration conducts its self I am just amazed . How they have been conducting policy is no less then shocking , they must be having some kind of lame contest as in who can out do the last totally lame person that has gone on to demonstrate the most ignorant thing possible. I am sorry but there is not words that can describe how so much has been taken for granted , and how disrespectful towards the people that have lived , fought , and died for this country, are remembered or treated, by this administration.

President Bill Clinton also bares responsibility he ended a war with out rendering its war lord / dictator responsible , for the acts he carried out.   I am not pro war by any account but when you have to defend against a aggressor , and you just let him get away with it , what was the thought , that all was forgiven , lets give him another chance at what, making a bigger problem. Well he certainly showed that he would , than he was made a martyr when he was strung up to the highest tree . Yeah that's the way to do it just pour gasoline on the fire, it will make for a block party weenie roast. I think that that George W. Bush and his gang of idiots must really like comedy movies , they must have watched the big block buster dumber and dumber and took it to hart , and said this is what were going to do to make a profit, if we just act dumber and dumber no one can say we deliberately planned the chain of events that are going to make us billions of dollars.

143

However maybe they really are that stupid , and if that's the case , that really is frightening that our leaders are like comedians that are behaving as retarded people do. Well what makes me say such a thing , how about our commander and chief is illiterate , or the vice president shoots his friend with a shot gun thinking he was a duck, yes that's right it really did happen. What's even more scary is that 50% of the American population voted for those ass holes, twice.

The United States has not had a educated President since Jimmy Carter and that was like almost 30 years ago, and the U.S. has suffered ever since. When Reagan got elected that was the beginning of the end , deregulation went into effect ,that's what started all that has accumulated to bringing our country to its knees , and led to the suffering that is now going on. I'll bet the people that elected him were quite proud of them selves, I am sure that the Devil was, he must be looking up and saying to God , I told you I would get back at you .

Chapter 14. Total abuse of power

Not since the United States liberated itself from British rule has there been such a runaway abuse of power that has taken over this country. This effect has transgressed into a breakdown of society itself, and has caused almost all industry's and or institutions to have been compromised, both corporally and idealistically. Its form is carried forward by the unsuccessful plan of deregulation however the only thing that deregulation accomplished was devolution.

It started from the top and with a simultaneous effect of ideology , infected all forms of society like the a pelage. Its aim was to un-restrict big business , that was not hard it influenced congressional leaders. The trickle down effect of deregulation then went after and conquered urban middle class as well as , inner city upper middle, church , state , independent you name it , and that once everybody was on board, it went as far as it could , until it caught up with its self , and finally sank the U.S. economy.

It did serve one purpose well , and that was it made everyone rich at the top of the economic chain , leaving everyone one and everything else to fend for its own. The ultimate pyramid scam.

At this point economic injustice settles in , and the first to feel the effect are the week , or powerless, rising health and cure costs overwhelmed society, when everything goes into the deregulation mode , all forms of quality control for health , food , medicine , environmental , transportation the very life blood of what societies are compromised, and any regard for integrity of such systems are abandoned , due to no money and or a lack or desire to have integrity perused. The trickle down effect is staggering , and has crippled all forms of society that due not have a understanding of such causes and effects. If some kind of integrity task force is not implemented on a global basis it will only get worse and that further complications will arise. The effect is similar as to how the virus anthrax is spread it comes from animals defecating on the ground that is walked on routinely , it is pounded into dust , the dust is kicked up , than inhaled by its victims. This dust must be neutralized or it will not stop the spread of this airborne contamination to life. However if the effected dust is made and spread out of ignorance and its victims are not made aware of such a thing , the cycle will continue and become more pronounced. This is the main problem if people new they were dyeing because of their sanitation habits they might have the ability to stop such a thing , but if they have been so brainwashed that they are not concerned and continue despite knowledge that would prevent the spread then this most likely is because the situation is so bad and hopeless that they no longer care for life, and that this does occur, especially when a greater power has forced people to live like animals in refuge style encampments and or unsanitary conditions from natural disasters and war.

Pretty disgusting wouldn't you say , the problem is that it does not stop there , other complexities arise, and or disease and virus's are generated, mutations that become stronger as their resistance to cure is inhibited by strengthening over time, its genetically induced the same way a animal or plant is genetically made resistant to disease or environmental conditions from breeding techniques.

Society has been robbed of its true patriotism because of desperation , fear , peer pressure, confusion , the media , especially in the United States or any country where the TV is a influential and biased form of culture. I guess that sums up our culture and what it has amounted to. I thank God that my father often cursed at the television when a obvious form of brain washing was taking place. I used to think it was funny when I was younger, that my father would swear and mock such things , I thought it was just a joke, and that he was just in a complacent mood. I know now that he was looking at the big picture.

The U.S. culture has gone thru many different forms and changes over the years, we are currently and have been since the Reaganomics era completely absorbed with the media hype coming from the TV. It is controlling our country and has perverted the true meaning of art and culture, to the point that it has been shaped by the advertising, company's that are in league with big business. I call it the dumbing down of society, it is really bad in places like Mexico. Ignorance is a breeding technique , just like intelligence , it must be taught and retained then exercised to further refine it , or make it more perfect.

When it has reached its pinnacle of success I just want to throw a boulder at the TV , or throw it out the window of a high building. That reminds me of a British rock band that did such things back in the 1970's , they were one of the most famous / controversial bands that came from England , and they stayed at a hotel that was not the most expensive one in town when they were here in L.A. however they were allowed to throw TV's out the windows , and that people thought they were great because of it , I know I did. The important thing was why they were throwing those TV's out the windows, they were demonstrating their opinion of the media in how it was a bad or ridicules effect on people , and that true art did not come from the TV. They know who they were and I thank them for doing so.

Conformance is achievable subliminally the big advertising company's spent millions of dollars on this technique , and perfected it in the 1960's and have been raking in the money ever since. Reality has become a virtual reality for most people, in that they would never hope to aspire to their true desires so they settle for someone acting it out on TV , on a daily or weekly basis. The soap operas that were to me a joke back in the 60's when they first came out became a emotional reality for mostly woman, at that time and that there expectations of life became shaped on such standards on many occasions.

This transferred into what they might expect from their spouses , and the trickle effect was started , the true origin of deregulation , big business , this caused the Men to have to compete with a virtual reality in trying to satisfy their mate's , this became a very controversial subject and that a sub-culture was started to combat such idealistic views. These sub-cultures were labeled occult's , secret societies , and even considered evil and or witch craft by some. The truth is that they were the reverent ones with respect to God , life , culture , true art.

They were engaged in a cultural revolution that was part of the things that were good about what was in the world. You could say it was the hippy generation that opened the eyes of a lot of people , and that they were mostly educated collage kids , just trying to make difference. The people that are now 50 to 60 years old know what I am talking about and if some of you kids these days have parents , that are my age , you should talk to them about what went on then and what is going on now , because the similarities are Identical except for the computers and technology. By the way for all you .com kids out there that think your smart , I'd like to see any of you accomplish now what we did back then with out computers, believe me what makes a person smart is what you can accomplish with primitive tools , and I mean primitive compared to what you have as a arsenal of tech. these days.

The fact is if integrity was not maintained back then we could not have done the things we did. That goes for every form of industry, Aerospace , Music , film , chemical refinement , machine , and manufacturing processes. Anybody can get it right using a computer, try it with out one , the computer makes it perfect no mistakes , back in the day you had to get it right with out a computer , and the equipment that was utilized was not even accurate or close to what would be considered today's standards.

The thing is we did do it , and we did peruse the inventions that are taken for granted in today's societies. While technology was progressing the business man , and woman , and political entities de-evolved and had taken everything we worked for and flushed down the toilet, talk about stupid. Our oceans are completely contaminated, as well as our land masses , air , and cities.

If anybody is thinking that God is going to come and destroy the world , so we can all be born again, you better think up a different scenario ,why would the creator be a destroyer , that's what he put the devil here for to assist us in accomplishing such a thing. It was not his idea for us to turn into a bunch of greedy ass holes. He gave us a semi perfect world and we did nothing but screw it up good, so take that to your Sunday church meeting and chew on it.

With that said lets talk about the religious abuse of power, one of my favorite all time subjects. I 'am not anti religion however I am anti hypocrite. True religion is as worth while a good cause if there ever was, however distortions , and prejudices have produced the worst effects that could be possibly contemplated. In that the most honorable causes were in the name of religious equality , some of the worst holocausts were driven from distorted leaders conveying a message that convinced people to strike down their fellow man in the name of such a cause , and or leave important decisions that should have clearly been thought out and not left to be of a spiritual interpretation.

Many times when things that take place because of a natural occurrence , and or unforeseen events taking place have been dismissed as Gods will. There is no such thing there is a reason for everything including Gods will, and that there is not a un-known reason for things that take place. Most things that happen that are un-desirable is because no one had the desire to foresee , contemplate , look at history , take into consideration , have the respect for danger that is existent and inevitable. This is basic nature and that everything that lives or flourish's is susceptible to

149

death and or corruption. It has always been this way and always will be. We can only cheat death for as long as the average person or animal can , none of us has ever out done anybody in this respect as far as a ultimate average is concerned no matter how , smart , or rich we are.

It all only lasts a certain amount of time, so what really matters is what you do while you are here. Today's goals are to see who can come up with the latest hype accelerators that will target mainstream populations , this is devised to stop and hinder , any and all forms of anti dumbing down. This is modern day socialistic communism that prays on the masses that are not aware of such endeavors.

Its real purpose is to strike a blow at true patriotism and or innovation / constructive evolution in the daily requirements of our planets needs, that would further humanism for the benefit of those in need . This type of abusive brainwashing has gone way further than anyone was willing to foresee by our world leaders ,however they really never were concerned. If they really were concerned they would have proved it with a more conservative approach to our environment , while demonstrating a more liberal attitude towards the upholding of ideas that would have been more conducive to our planets need's.

That goes on to say that in our country what has been practiced and has led to things getting to this point 10-03-08 in the financial / political world that has become the central focal point , is very simply the good cop , bad cop routine.

This concept has been around way before Hollywood used it for theatrical exploit's , very simply the republicans are the bad cop's in that they want to take down the criminal and or rough him up, and the democrats are the good cops saying to the criminal now look you must cooperate or my partner is going to get nasty about this and he is not as nice as me, so just tell us what we want before its to late.

The criminal however is not a criminal he is you and me , and the only thing we were guilty of is letting these political 1930's style corrupt cops take over , well they have the guns , lawyers , and money so what's new what can we do. I'll tell you what we do don't cooperate, how can you go to jail because they made you poor , and sick, and unable to sustain under their interpretation , what's a credit rating who's credit rating , who are these credit institutions that have all the money to judge you , who's judging them, what standard did they live up to.

The government need's to assign them a credit rating based on their failure to deliver a comprehensible system of business . They started all this, it evolved by their hands choking the life out of everyone just to make a profit.

The point is the two cops had this worked out ahead of time and manipulated the unsuspecting person being interrogated. It works often enough and that the cops had done as much as they could, to for fill there job performance. This is there excuse for saying they have done as much as they could , when things don't work out then they start pointing fingers at each other saying its his fault , no its his , you should have said this or done that, and then that's it , end of story the repubs and the dems have done there duty and its time for the next case.

This is fine for cops or Hollywood movies but this is no way to run a country. The only thing that comes to mind when I see how our political system works is that the elected office members have been watching to many B movies and not looking at what's going on in the real world, and or what's worse they could care less.
Chapter 15   Two party's one agenda your money

The function of the two major political parties is mostly based on how much money they can appropriate. This appropriated money is

151

all at the expense of the majority of the people in this country who make less than $100,000. a year, that's 95% of the population. However they have none of the voice on what's going to happen to them because of runaway government policy's. They have been led into a false sense of everything is going to be alright because big brother is watching over you. Well big brother was watching but not with the people's best interest. They were concentrating on getting you , your money , and what ever other purpose would suite their agenda's. If you don't think they planned all this than , why is it happening its not just some accident or misfortunate effect , when all the institution's become corrupt , or insolvent. These practices have been exercised for hundreds of years , and wide open since reganomics unleashed unrestricted deregulation practices.

Devolution then had set in and has been working it's ill fated fault's ever since. Once a cultural mainstream shift occurs it is almost impossible to reverse the trend due to the passing of generation's that have been involved with all aspects of established modern value's. This makes it very difficult for anyone to properly definerate the difference between basic Democratic / Republican party ideals in that they have become more like each other. I personally do not support the idea of having different political parties because of such effects that are translated into the mainstream to confuse and disadvantage the average person.

It's hard enough to comprehend the difference's for the average people , and that at one point it becomes a popularity contest and not what the original intention of selective idea's are meant to be interpreted as. This point is elaborated on by the following condition's that would support my view.

The elderly population will vote for the elderly because they can relate to them on a age basis, and or the calm demeanor.

The Younger crowd will vote for the younger politicos based on relating to them, and there promises of a future that will have their interest's.

This is not necessarily bad , but it is not how our political elected officials should be voted on ,and or their qualifications determined on the running of this country compared with key issues that do not get conveyed due to over generalizing of a running platform. This is not obligating the running party to adhere to promises in policy that would be the basis for their critique over their opponent. In stead they have reduced the platform they are running, based on what the competitor does not do and or their short coming's, in that it might be true what is noted of their opponent , it does not elaborate on their views or make them better, based on their critiques.

This has evolved into a social society of finger pointer's and that the end result is nothing changes or has evolved in the right direction. This demeanor of current society roll playing has and continues to turn everyone against the other for mostly the purposes of self worth and carrier acceleration , this type of attitude is prevalent in today's U.S. society and has become the major platform for advancement due to a subculture that is now in place thru the use of practice's that are recognized as socially expectable.

This aggressive and non-integrity based ideology is a big problem and that in my belief it has dominated much of today's thinking in the corporate and government institutions.

I have done some research into this area and found the following institutions to be caught up into this corrupt way of thinking , and that job performance has been compromised. I attribute this to be prevalent due to improper leadership.

Elected officials most all branches of government , foreign or domestic, Government workforces (US / MEXICO) FAA, DOD , DOT, FEMA , NASA , FBI , CIA , Homeland Security, Local &

Federal Police , Department of Agriculture , All levels of large corporation companies , most levels of medium size corporations, All Airline company's foreign or domestic , Immigration , School's all level's, Banking institution's , all level's & or insurance / finance company's, food , & chemical .

As you can see this problem is wide spread and because of it being so wide spread it is more than fair to recognize it as a cultural problem of mass proportion , anyone seeking job placement in these areas should be advised that there are effects that will be felt by any one trying to excel in endeavors covered by the listed subject's Up to now the seriousness of this lack of integrity in respect to job and or skill performance has not been properly evaluated , and that it is eroding not only at all the plant's and animal's , but causing irreversible damage to our land and ocean's.

The leaders of all the major country's have been alerted and informed of the listing mentioned , but fail to act responsibly on the required topic's as to not cause a furtherance of such problematic effect's. I am truly afraid that if this trend continues there will be nothing left , but a total up heaval and destruction to everything on this planet. This is a very serious subject and it is in the hands of our elected officials to do what is needed to stop the insanity of what's going on. There must be a integrity taskforce assigned to each institution that is considered deficient in the monitoring and or holding of their own Quality Assurance system that is not performing , further more any deficits in the effects that are the result from such non-performance must be dealt with in a fair and reasonable amount of time that would not further such effects and or cause damage that would be irreversible. There must also be put into place such task forces , for agency's that have not been created yet and that such agency's that relate to the stopping of pollution's and or contamination's to the earth's environment's must be put into place. This must be done due to the increase of population growth , and the diminishing natural resource's that are in continues deficit due to the population uses across this planet.

154

The United Nations is a good example of a system of country's that could be considered a federation for the conservation of natural recourses of this planet and that the bigger the country , the more financial responsibility should be assigned . This financial responsibility should be enforced onto the corporations and or government institution's that are causing the problem's and or deficits, regardless of any reason what so ever.

There must be a intellectually understanding with all the major country's as to what the origin of true evil is and that there focus must be maintained toward the non-hypocritical truth of such a understanding. That truth being the world will die before any kind of human anileation thru the use of military force. The Idea that a small or rouge nation that does not have the ability to compete with all the NATO super powers is ridicules, and that such propaganda that would be propounded by any government agency should be securitized to find out who would be responsible for perpetrating such non-sense or lies for personnel gain, that includes all elected officials and or dictators of government's, Including the United States of America, first and foremost due to the fact that the U.S. is financially responsible to the world, they must be also responsible for up holding the integrity , and self integrity to higher standards then anyone else regardless as to what they have done in the past.

Financial superiority in this day and age spells control of power not just wealth and that with much power comes much corruption of power , and that a integrity task force is required for such power more so then any other country , this is also the basis and substantiation that would lead the rest of the world by demonstrating by example and leave nothing to be questioned on the motives for such act's.

It has been demonstrated that as of 10-03-08 the United States has shown to be out of control for their monetary institution's and that this has caused a deficit to other country's around the world. This is the same sort of problem that fueled WWII , and that if we are not careful from now on, it could start another major conflict, this is not something that has been brought up by the mainstream media, at this time however there are many historians that can point out from recorded history that such things were the making's of world wars.

These policy's must be pursued if the world has any chance of righting it self from all the negligence that has gone on for so many years. It must be achieved from the ground up, the people that are going to do the work have to have a reason self sustainment would be such a reason in that the poor have the most to loose or have lost the most so far , there for they would be the best suited to take on the responsibility for such endeavors. They also would be critical on big business in that they are not a part of it nor have they benefited from it.

Integrity must be promoted and rewarded / respected and that if such a system of checks and balance's is to be viable than protection will also be needed against corrupt forces that would tend to try and prevail. This is a major deterrent in most economic and or organizational society's , this integrity must be further maintained as to not have everything that was worked for only disrupted by the threat of greed and corruption. This is the major problem within all society's in that ultimate security of integrity must be a major priority and not a minor one. If the changing of the millennium has taught us one thing it has made a big impression that for safety of society as well as integrity to financial and ecological consideration's are all equally important subject's to be of concern. This has been elaborated on by one leading democratic party leaders on 10-03-08 in that she stated accountability must be maintained from this point on and that the average citizens rights and values must be the concern of this administration and or others to follow in the future. OK then miss speaker I hope you know what it means as to what your saying because at this point the

156

American people as well as the world have probably had as much hypocrisy as their going to take .

This is a monumental task and that the complexity of it is no small effort it drives to the very core of humanism as it is known. The Idea is simple however it is not so simply achieved, due to the size and magnitude of such a endeavor. The people that have made the problems of the world are not going to go away , so we must get used to dealing with their miss guided ideals. Since they are not aware of how sick they are , and the American public is equally as miss guided obviously they elected them in to power that they have wielded for the past 30 or more years it only stands to reason it might take as long to straighten out such a mess, however we might not have that much time so we better get things moving on a faster track.

There's been a lot of damage done , and the amount of inter agency's and task force personnel are going to be enormous, however this will cause a lot of jobs to take place and that the effect of correcting such a problem will generate and contribute to a economy of domestic work force to take place. Country's that are not inclined to participate should be cut off from importing their products to this country, it does not mean they will be sanctioned from receiving or importing in a general way but in a specific way that will leave the discrepant country to right their own solution in that they will not other wise
profit from selling our country their merchandise (this should be limited by a particular society of business as to not let anyone who is upholding integrity to suffer such as aerospace , or computer manufactures these would be considered separate society's based on engineering and production of such good's). Since the United States is the largest consumer of their products , and the most profitable investment of foreign funds due to our financial institution's that are unequalled anywhere in the world they will be forced to comply or not reap the benefit of their country's company's profiting so greatly with out being part of U.S. led financial order.

This is the true purpose of deregulation in what it should stand to accomplish that would force the corruption from settling in , and this form of free trade will take care of it's self , somewhat like deregulation had in mind except instead of the object of its purpose to be of generating money as its primary purpose , the object of purpose would be of the Idea of a purpose without corruption, as the primary reason of its purpose. This is the only deregulation that will benefit this or any other country.   Free trade is a good Idea but it is not free , some one has to be responsible as to the free trade that would go is fare trade.

Chapter 16   The Effect

The global effect that is felt when the U.S. is in deficit of banking or
moralistic value is phenomenal to most people and that they had no
idea of such effects that would be felt and reverberated thru out the
world. In that the U.S. population feels the effect, foreign country's
population's are also equally effected. This is proof that the U.S.
economic structure feeds the world's banking institution's and that
for the most part foreign effects felt will be of the higher Asian class
and general European population's & Some higher class of Russian
as well.

In as much as those multi million dollar company's that have
attributed if not formed the cause of current economic and
moralistic devaluation, and very well deserve any short coming's
from it , they are not going to be affected. It un-fairly hurt's the
working class they do not have millions of dollars tucked away to
get thru this problem that was caused by big money. They will
loose what little they have , and or will not have the opportunity to
have anything because of such things that have gone on. This is the
nature of the game. It always has been , and always will be the only
benefit would be that the poor get a harsh lesson on basic
economics' if they even can comprehend why this is happening to
them.

It is amazing to me the amount of middle class Americans that don't
understand any of this, they think that what happens on wall
street is not going to effect them , and there glad wall street is
having a problem.

That's because all they have herd is that it effect's wall street from
the television, and that there to busy hammering out a living and
that they don't even have the time to stop and take a look around

them as to what and why these things are taking place.
Even if they could comprehend the truth they would probably shrug
their shoulders and say well what can I do about it anyway. For the
most part they are right what are they going to do about it , it's a
chess game and the blue collar worker is the pawn. There are a few
things they could do about it but because of the laws that wont
protect them from big business monopolizing and capitalizing on
there ideas they are very limited.

When I was younger and I went out and competed with the world I
found that technological service's that utilized equipment made in
the U.S. was very expensive and logistically hard to support in
foreign country's. My father had helped me into such endeavors
that involved utilizing commercial Aircraft in foreign country's ,
work that he was famously involved with when he was my age at
the time, and that I got to see the world because of it.

That's where most of my knowledge comes from related to the
writings in this book that is based on international subject matter.
This was before wide spread computer utilization or the .com age ,
or the housing boom or any of that, back when the world was
somewhat predictable. However at the turn of the millennium I had
been pushed out of what I had worked hard for by people that would
use the American big business technique of use , analyze , and copy
with funding needed to achieve.

This is the main problem as soon as someone does something , all
someone else has to do is come along with more money and
capability and out you go. So I learned that no matter how hard you
work there is always someone there to take advantage of you , it
never fails. At this point it narrows down the possibility's of
achieving something with out the application of big business
involvement. This intern forces you to do something completely
different or original that would take some one no matter what a few
years to catch you. In the mean time to achieving this original idea
you have to sustain and with rising cost's and inflation , and getting

older , its just not as easy as it use to be, especially if you have been reduced to practically nothing at that point , so you have to literally start over, for most people this is impossible and they cannot do it. The only reason I am able to completely redefine my self is that when I was younger and a apprentice I never settled on being a conformist , even when I was offered a guaranteed income I felt that my freedom was worth more than any amount of money, and that my love for life and my hatred for repression would keep me going which it did.

It's very difficult now to keep this view point but my mother and my father installed this in me when I was young and it cannot be removed even if I try to and I have, I cannot. It is haunting and that for me to give in and say big money won would be the same as going to jail , and I was not built to be a prisoner of no man or woman.

We all have a choice in life and it takes gut's to make that choice, it does not come with out sacrifice , or hardship , nor will you be popular with certain critic's but one thing's for sure , the alternative no matter what is not the same, there must be nothing worse from what I have seen of people that have to say I should of tried to do this ,or I really wanted to do that, I can thank God that I am not one of them and that I might not have the wealth of others or the status and recognition they enjoy ,but I did have a life and it did not lack, I got to do all the things that big money people could not, no matter how much money they had , because you cannot buy everything with money , something's must be earned or they are not attainable.

Chance's must be taken we are all here because someone had taken a chance , our parent's for one ,if they did not we would not exist. They took a chance that they were as bold as the love they had for each other.

161

These are perceptions that shape our destiny , who we are, or who we are not , or what we would strive to be. If you give up on such thing's than you have compromised on what you aspire to be , and as Americans or any other human being born on this planet we have the right to be what we want , what we need, and what should be, our life's destiny that we planned out , and not what someone tried to force down our throat's. The truth is very simple you just have to recognize it. When you see it , your ambition will guide you.

There are still a lot of ways that young people can achieve today without the aid of corporate / big money if things are not done like clock work. There are also a lot of business and real-estate capability's due to people not being able to sustain their planned business because times got tuff for them and that the original lenders had been stuck with property or equipment that they must make liquid,   and if you have a way to work such thing's that can be your shot.

That's how I was able to get a chance at things it was at a time similar to now back in the late 1980's during the saving's and loan crisis and there were a few different bank's that had Aircraft equipment that they did not know what to do with so I told them I would put them to work and I did , it was not easy but I prevailed , and was successful in that I had the most important thing I needed to go forward and that was simply the persistence of taking a chance when one had arisen , and trying as hard as I could it worked while everyone around me was failing and said it was not a good Idea and lots of other skeptical thing's I ignored them , gave it a shot , and it worked.

At the same time I was able to save a elderly man's life savings of his house that he would have lost if I did not, he too was victim of someone talking him into investing in something that their was not a legitimate reason it would be successful. He had everything to loose if someone did not help him , I had nothing so I only risked the effect of getting in debt. I was able to pay down the debt of over $200,000. and became owner of 4 Aircraft , the elderly man did not loose his house , however the person that talked him into such a thing never risked anything and walked away with no responsibility just like big business , what a guy. I suppose he resented the Idea that he failed and I was successful , however the justification and the reward I enjoyed was being able to peruse a endeavor that made me feel proud of helping my self and at the same time someone that was a innocent victim.

The present effect of the world financial situation's is very close in proximity to the late 1980's and that I feel if people that are motivated by diminishing work from the corporate and big business centers exercised some of the similar techniques I have described they could come out of a bad situation with out a lot of financial pain. The key is people that are experts in their field must be empowered like I was for this to take place, and that if the banks have any sense of how their money was being generated legitimately they will recognize certain individual's to be of value that could exercise, their talent in the face of hopelessness, and that such individual's must stand up for themselves and not be taken in by the television or the other people that don't have the ability or sense to do anything else but repeat what they are fed by the media, and or other people that have no ambition.

The Government's that say they are in knowledge of how to deal with a situation that pertains to the average working place individuals are liars , there the one's that let this problem get out of hand , and the first thing they did is cower and help them selves. If the governments would have invested in their own country , and I am talking about the big 6 or 9 or what ever they call them selves , what a joke they are big now at being liars , traitor's , and coward's , and the whole world knows it because what's been done is now history , and it is not someone's opinion.   There are so many wasted opportunity's that the government's of the world had to do the right thing and they did not , they have failed us , just as they have in the past , they convinced everyone with this sense of just do what we say it will be OK we got it covered.

It is written in the bible that those that would be a false profit in his name would suffer the most, eternally. I am sure glad I never went around saying I do this or I do that in the name of God , and I am pretty sure that you can't go to hell based on talk alone , however the action's of these leader's that go on , are far from reverent especially if they are responsible for murdering hundred's of thousand's of innocent men , women , and children. In that case I don't think god is going to care how many more time's they would say god bless you , when all that they actually did was send all those people straight to hell in the name of god and the United States , well I am from the U.S. and I did not approve those murder's so I will decline on the god bless you's , thanks anyway.

What I don't understand is how they get away with it, this is the year 2008 isn't it ? , I can't believe that people still act this way. I have only one thing to say about all that to the world. Wake up !! do like Nancy Regan use to say , you remember" just say no" Just say no to murder , corruption , and sorry Nancy deregulation.

This whole thing has gotten way out of hand for to long ,if people with a conscious don't take control of this country I am afraid we have had it , as they say. The lack of integrity will prevail and then they will hit us again using our own lack of self respect and lack of security for our innocent citizen's . They have already proven they were willing to die for their cause , and with such a perseverance, in their mind , a purposeful sacrifice to god and family, so after we continued to bomb these peoples family's and the only thing left is their trust in what their family thought was god, that does not leave much to wonder about. Remember over 6,000 U.S. military personnel committed suicide in 2005 after they came back or while they were in Iraq doing what our government commanded them to do. The buck is going to stop somewhere , I hope it's not at my front door, and I fear for the American's that have been brain washed by the government's administration.

My grand children did not murder anyone and they don't want to, or understand why anyone would and they certainly don't deserve to suffer , like many other good American's, they do not need any part of this crap. When will the government stop such policy's that have a never ending cycle of death to the innocent , never have so many had to pay for so few to make a profit , it's just incredible . This is not the United State's that I grew up in , this administration does not make me proud of how our leaders are acting , it make's me ashamed .

It certainly does not exercise what is printed on our monetary note's (In God We Trust). The United State's is suppose to set a example to the rest of the world as to what is good about life , what gives hope to the repressed , we no longer as a society do that . The reason is that more than 50% of the people have voted into power , a administration that thinks they do not need to be on the alert for all the different form's of enemy's both foreign and domestic that would compromise this country's integrity.

There are million's of American's that died for this country in belief that their was integrity here , and that it was worth dying for , and this is how they are respected , by completely disrespecting their life's blood and sacrifice.

Yes I am ashamed and everyone that voted for our acting administration policy's should be. I did not that is something I am not ashamed of. This country has a responsibility to serve it's fallen patriot's , it's because of their sacrifice's that we can enjoy a safe and productive environment , it's because of their strength that we live. Who ever does not think so should leave this country and go some where else to live where such notion's are not part of their country's history and then tell me how you like it there , I guaranty they will come back to the United State's and kiss the ground while thanking god for giving them a second chance for redemption

We can not win a fight some where else if we don't have unity in our home sanctuary , it's just not done that way, we must be United here first so we have the ability to properly and legitimately have the capability in the eye's of the world and in our hart's to defeat our adversary's. There must be a noble and worth cause to achieve , look at history it has proven that arrogance never won the day anywhere , and that nobility and unity had always done so because it was a just cause, this is what empowers people, that is why the U.S., England , and Australia won WWII , against what were such great odds that would not have looked that way except for the fact that the cause was noble and everyone rallied in unity to it's call.

There was no Atom bomb dropped on Germany by England they conquered their enemy the old fashion way with nobility, and a little help from their friend's. The U.S. was delivering successful raid's onto Japan at the ending of the war, and that we would have prevailed no matter what , mainly due to the way the noble action's that soldiers fought with honor were carrying forward. The Atom bomb was not needed we were going to win regardless it would have only taken a few more weeks or month's and that would have been it, instead they used the bomb and fed the nuclear race ever since , this gave all the country's of the world a reason to fear after that.

Most of the people killed by the nuclear attacks were civilian's , woman , children, wounded , & elderly, it was detonated directly over a hospital and small single family dwelling's with wooden roofs and that there was no significant military advantage to this. This was due to a wind direction that was not contemplated from the altitude of the plane that dropped the first one. Most of the military were out on the ocean or in the bay and or on what was left of their navy's fleet and were not killed or injured . (reference

166

Hiroshima John Hersey) Pulitzer Prize-winning author that went to Japan and recorded his findings just days after the holocaust had taken place.

Other references include USAF photographic aircraft that accompanied the lead aircraft Enola Gay that dropped the first bomb. The decision for this came from the President of the United States. Over 200,000 people were killed between the two bombs that were dropped because of the emperor of Japan , like Sadam Husane made the innocent victims of that country responsible for his arrogance and corruption. Upon interviewing victim's of the bombing of Japan and asked how they felt about the whole thing many responded that it was expected and that there society up to that point held the emperor of Japan as a great leader and that this was taught to them since child hood to think that way , along with their duty to commit suicide when required to keep honor for their family and country.

A perfect example of how a honorable culture was manipulated for the purpose of their leader to exalt himself as a greater then life figure , not unlike Hitler , or Sadam Husane, and to further clarify a race driven to prevail with out proper justification. A clear case of the perverted and sick leading the blind and or submissive and un-educated or fearful.

The action's of a repressed country by the leader's of that country should not justify the killing of innocent civilian's , this is not what the United States is suppose to stand for, it certainly does not define Christianity. A important point is that when the U.S. act's in this fashion we or any other country that would do so are not setting the example that God demonstrated as a base to go by , and for a society to use such a base and act in discordance with that ,only implies the hypocritical aspect's of our leader's . Our country is comprised of many different nationality's and that this mentality is no longer viable and puts all Americans at risk of self disintegrity of

167

what we are suppose to stand for. This is not good P.R. and it might
lend to why this country is having a massive melt down in the
integrity department.

God help us were going to need it, from what I can see so far, let's
hope the next administration can fair a little better at getting the
people to have a little more unity, we have not learned much in the
past 60 years that would demonstrate otherwise based on the
action's of this administration, The middle east was never
a threat anything like Japan , Germany , or Russia and in all reality
we used a sledge hammer on a cockroach , the same job could have
been accomplished with proper timing at the time when Iraq was the
aggressor during the first Gulf war and at least the people would
have understood why they were being blasted back to the stone
age instead we waited a complete generation, why ? , this type of
confusion only breed's fanatic's , and that the lack of self discipline
did not help protect us either , people paid
tax's to the government and all their high tech contractors , that
could not even perform basic security at public airports .

If it was not so sad it would be a joke, but it's not a joke and a lot of
innocent people died because their was not anybody excepting
responsibility in the government's administration (see the 911
commission report). Then we still did not learn , and our entire
monetary infract structure and moralistic values were flushed
down the toilet by the same administration policy's.   WHATS
NEXT ? Is the president of the United States going to get on
national television and say to everyone OK everybody its time to
drink the cool aid , all together now. The main stream media must
be in league with the government because nothing is being said or
done to combat this lack of integrity. It is continually ignored on a
daily basis as if its not important , or somebody else's problem.

Well it's not somebody else's problem it's every Americans and
there responsibility to stop this repetitive lack of integrity , but yet

nothing is accomplished. We don't even have any viable subculture's anymore because they can not afford to live in major city's or be at a advantage to do much. That's why this problem must be addressed at a federal level and that there must be accountability agency's put into place that can fund such program's. We use to have many such program's in this country but they have been stamped out by the wastefulness of the government and their selective subculture of corruption.

There is a extreme amount of brainwashing that is accompanying the arrogance and corruption that is down playing anyone trying to say or do anything ,this is also apparent in our culture at all levels and age group's. As far as the younger generation they are from what I have seen completely un-rebellious in this respect and merely make up their own rules that are not much different then what the offender's are doing in that they acknowledge their own peer groups to work with , that do not change anything but only try to cover each other's tracks in what seems to be a culture caught up in compliance and deception of true feeling's towards their situation.

This is due to fear , fear from their parent's , or their peer's , or even worst the people in their own age group who they wish to gain acceptance with. This disingenuous form of living is poisoning their brain washed mind's, and it does not promote innovative thinking what so ever. This in turn restricts their adherence to only current excepted system's , mostly big business , government , and already well established company's that are way to big for their own good. This is causing a deficit in qualified individuals that can perform the required innovation's that are required for the advancement of a population that is growing way to fast for their respective societies needs. Other examples of this effect are given by looking at all the outsourcing to foreign country's that are now producing the required equipment we do not produce in this country. We are suppose to lead not follow and because of the manufacturing infrastructure that is becoming less existent this is no longer the

169

case for the things that are required for this country to be non-dependent on less stable or quality maintained product's.

This effect is being transmitted not only in manufacturing but in the food , textile's , chemical , and all other form's of commodity's that are imported to this country. As you can see the simple effect that greed inspires forces a complex array of problem's to arise in our culture and or material requirement's. The result is disease , poverty , human right's abuse, and so on, none of which should be tolerated by this country , and if people do not take up their voice and elaborate on the problem's it will get worse , because it will transfer even more so to foreign country's and the translating effect will come back to the U.S.

People want to blame other's for there problem's and the way that is done these days is that the people with the most , will get the most blame even if it is not true or that , the people with the most really don't have the most and this was just a product of their own propaganda , the unsuspecting don't understand this and the problem has reversed and backfired. Much like the current financial situation , where everybody wants to blame wall street , for the problem and they might be the benefactors from the problem , it was not carried out by them , it takes a army to thrust out such a assault .

It was carried forward by the subordinates for the most part and the lack of smart judgment by the customer's , just like any other assault. It will take that same amount of force to reverse such an assault. Regardless of who was in charge who headed such a thing. Remember it is soldiers that carry out the battle only under the direction of the generals. So I guess we need some generals that are not corrupt. Those are suppose to be our elected politicians, so we better get a movement together or its not going to happen. It should not be hard to find them they would stand to do well if they are a minority and all the rest are corrupt, that would make them unique

170

and a valued commodity in a world that is sinking from the other.

Corrupt politicos are a surplus commodity at this point there are to many of them and they are starting to challenge them selves for their territories not un-like the drug cartels that are fighting over their territories. They will self deplete eventually but at what cost to innocent people are effected is the problem.

Chapter 17 Expectations crises

There are far to many people that expected way to much to do much less than the value for their existing ability's , and that by doing so , there must be a reciprocal that would be on the other end of the company spectrum. That reciprocal is the blue collar worker , the basic soldier in the field carrying out the most dangerous work , their scenario is very similar. They are paid the least , get none of the benefit's , and or required health benefit's to enable them to excel if they even survive their primary job requirement of the entry level they begin at.

The whole design of the thing limit's there excelling , and that the executive position starts out at where any of the entry position's would hope to attain , after a life time of servitude. This is why thing's are out of balance , it has become very easy for most middle class family members or (higher class family member's) to attain a executive position right out of the gate. I am not referring to a engineering and or technical physics position and or work description , because those areas of expertise are a carrier description that requires true knowledge , and not just the ability to operate a computer , look at pie chart and then copy / paste their way to success.

There is a huge deficit for the qualified personnel that could fill the empty job's needed at this time. Those company's are not laying off their key personnel they need more , and are missing thousand's.

A big problem that was shown in a drastic financial way that caused the banking crises is that there were to many un-qualified position manager's, that were responsible for running / oversight for those company's that did not do a proper job in their required area.

That's a example and not a exception of the U.S. cultural awareness of today's main work forces in the key management / executive position's. This also extends to the rest of the country's of the world it's not a U.S. phenomena , its just that our banks happen to guide the rest of the world based on the U.S. stock market. Think about it if we don't have people in this country that will do something at a fair price the executive big plan is down size and silently import from a foreign country and that is what's been happening for a long time now in this country.

The executive plan does not call for retraining American's or tax allowance's to be a incentive , they have their off shore account's and they are masters at dodging tax's they have a lot of ivy league grads. that went to collage to learn how to perfect industrial tax evasion , after all when everything is said and done it all comes down to tax's , and the more they get out of paying the less the government has to give to the needy. It's the trickle effect that the politico's don't want to talk about in their deregulated plan's , it's their secret , well it's not that much of a secret anymore the cats out of the bag , and it's running around all over the place , and does not no where it is , and that's because their little subculture is turning on it's self to survive or make a profit , this is where they separate the old and the wise from the corrupt novice, or the fat cat from the small kitten.

You can look at just about any industry and find these claims to be true , what is so ridicules is that these company's should have at least one employee that knows what he is doing so at least they have a Idea of what they can get away with and what is cutting their own throat , or maybe they do and the executives are ignoring and hoping for the best , probably the latter is 99% of the scenario's.

A pronounced and large number of the contributing culture damage comes from the mid level , these executives have a culture of miniaturized work ethic's fault that is circulated to all the

173

participant's of their level , this is not new but your basic entry level exec is expecting more these days , and they are just organized to culturize their system , this because the fat cats have taught them this and that they have bred this culture to take place , it was inevitable with deregulation making it possible to teach and enhance such a sub-division of ethic's to take place. It has taken many years to evolve and that what had taken place is because of timing , technology , current world affairs , political administrations through out the world , a new world disorder you could say .

Every 20 years this cycle repeats in the U.S. the last time was the late 1980's , before that it was the late 1960's , in Europe it was the 1940's mostly because of the same effect's that prevailed in the U.S. during the 60's / 80's , this effect was most pronounced by the resultant post war institutional economic plan's that limited Germany and Japan as to what they would be allowed and what they would not be allowed to produce such as cars, motorcycle's , motion picture camera's , the soft product's.

Japan it was electronics , high quality refined steel for bearing's , fishing net's. These were Ok'ed by the U.S. and part of the surrender plan, imposed onto the people and the culture as defined by the allies , you will do what we say , you are allowed to do and you will not be allowed to evolve or build Ship's , airplane's , rocket's , or any of the technical oriented hardware device's of that time period's history, in as much as they submitted to their respected Hitler / Emperor they were after that war in submission to the allies rules.

This was highly contested by the Christian's of those country's , and that they viewed it as the same living condition's of their previous dictator's , communism and it was. This was part of a theological effect that was being used by the allies , and that this same effect was considered relevant in the dropping of the Atomic bomb's over Japan. The allies took advantage of a massive brainwashing of their own design after the war and used this as a

174

safety precaution that would prevent a resurgence of hostility to re-take place. However or whatever their reasons were it did transmit into a economic portfolio that the allies designed and that the high quality product's that were constructed by these people's was undermining their very existence, however nobody might have guessed how profiesiant there capability's would develop into , and that the U.S. had actually driven those country's into becoming the most financially successful culture's per capita in the world. Here again is a example that is not being set properly and kept generation's of innocent civilian's from being able to develop their capability's because of their previous corrupt leaders. This too is not what the United States is suppose to stand for.

If history is examined thoroughly it shows how all the worst things in a culture and or it's leadership stems from greed and corruption and that the subjects of the country's involved are further dismayed by the totalitarian leaders that seem to be larger than life , in that they command the very infrastructure for the existence of the respective cultures. There is no such thing as a entire culture that believed they were a master race or sent by God to defeat evil or a list of other bogus theme's , they were taught and bread into these society's for lack of a better example, and our response to such a problem was to make them think the same about the U.S.

Our reason for this was to ensure or safety. What I would like to know is why we did not ensure our safety before things were left to get out of hand and to escalate to a point of the resulting wars. From what I get from history being the mirror of our cultural soul, as all this came into play so perfect it could not have been choreographed better if the leading business men of the day planned all the delayed responses ,and missed opportunity's to safe guard the innocent members of society ?, Ironic isn't it how such thing's come to be, by the few that profit the most.

History is not a theory it is a fact of physics as to what had taken place, and the main contributor to all the different opinion's come from religion. and culture   This comes into play when certain cultures are evaluated by the greater powers using the so called guilty society's cultural attributes to judge them. It must be understood that there is no such thing as a true culture in respect to a super power or world leader force , that's because what ever culture was being developed was the permitted culture of that country's leader and all the leaders were going for the glory, regardless if they had a legitimate reason, including the USA.

Probably the example that stands out the best in respect to the U.S. would be the invading and conquering of the American Indians after the the desisting of English rule , in that it was justified to kick the corrupt British leadership out, the U.S. turned around and did what they wanted with the American Indian's and or the Mexican Indian's, and they were considered the minority's as far as U.S. culture was concerned. My point is people that live in glass houses should not throw stones in it, and should not support stone throwing as it's primary policy because broken glass will be inevitable.

If our God was the true example we should have acted in accordance with those teaching's as a culture , as to avoid being looked upon as   hypocrite's of a society , because history is what is looked upon and what will show and or teach the world , to ignore these teachings , is to ignore the very existence that the educated world has been pursuing since Aristotle , the first person that is known to record and analyze history and or psychological awareness in the time period 350BC , ancient Greece , in that his basic teachings are considered relevant in all of modern society's of today , through out the modern world.

Today's mind set is so incredible as to what people that are the so called educated think and demand that they are worth , compared to the reality of the situation that it is no wonder that the costs of everything has gotten to the point it is. This goes for everything that is particularly located in the major city's where just the opposite should be true for costs associated due to the mass amounts that are used and sold in these city's. This is attributed to the amount of immigrant's that don't know the value's , and will pay whatever it cost's because they are forced into the situation based on risking everything they had just to get here , and then not having a choice in how to deal with their option's other then people already here in that they will have confidence with contact's they feel comfortable with. These immigrant's contribute to the way price's are inflated because of supply and demand being based on readily available , as the supply , and taking what is prepared, as the demand.

The people that have taken advantage of this , in collusion with the bank's, is why the current administration had done virtually nothing to stop the flow of immigrant's, they were bolstering the economy, in a quick buck way . This gave everybody a sense of economic euphoria, until September of 2008, when it all caught up. Now everyone act's like they did not know why this happened , yeah sure they didn't , they planned it , how could they not. At the same time the quick buck syndrome was taking place big business manufacturing company's were gearing up to go into full swing to get on the massive military contract's / civil contracts that were taking place. The only problem they don't have qualified management , engineering , technical , laboratory technicians that are needed to fulfill contract's and order's that are way behind , because of qualified personnel , the main problem is that as a society we promoted just the opposite the past 8 year's in that people were inclined to not want a technical knowledge compared with living the easy and fast life that was promoted. The effect of all these factor's resulted in a moralistic breakdown in real values , this will force the U.S. company's to take well educated people from foreign country's if they want to survive, and be able to get through this , if they can. The existing technician's will be put on stressful condition's in order to satisfy the company leaders , this will not work.

177

The good thing from all this will be that for the first time in a long time a blue collar , and or professional technicians will be worth what they do. This will not happen to quickly but in the coming month's the wait and see method that executives are used to using will fail and that their only way to go will be to pay the people what they are worth so they have a motive to get educated and start being productive to the extent of having enough productive personnel.

This was inevitable but it is reassuring that personnel suppliers are motivated to seek individual's that have a capability to produce what is needed. We will return to a industrialized nation and that it will be based on doing as much as possible in a intelligent way that will guaranty banks that their investment's will have a predictive return , and the only thing that does that will be for the most part government backed or highly successful private ventures with real solid asset's that are liquid, and industrialized based , just like they now have in China , the
way used to have in this country before the business man sold us out.

The U.S. government has run a muck (oct. 2008) the only thing they could think of right off the bat was to cripple the banks into a freezing of their profit generating capability from a financial institution point of view , there answer is selling short term treasury bonds , and that the buyers are using these bonds to escape the bankruptcy of failing banks because the treasury simply prints as much money as needed to do what ever they want. This does not fix a problem it creates one if the government loans money to the failing banks and the failing banks investors pull their investments out from being backed by the government , and then the government says there will be no flip around trading but in fact that is what the government is doing that very thing over a time period of every thirty days , well the only thing I see is the chicken lays a bunch of eggs , and now who feeds the little chickens when they hatch if there is no food. There is no accountability in this method of controlling our monetary system. All this does is give the largest company's and investment security's a guaranty of success regardless of what causes anything to happen.

The present Treasury secretary with the help of the federal reserve bank are insanely running a muck, and playing God with the future of not just the US but the world. Both present administration's are guilty of letting them do this although one of them is defiantly to blame for causing the situation . In that the Treasury print's as much money as is required , this does nothing for the consumer's at the bottom of the system, the money that's printed and distributed is only divided into the top banks and richest people in the system, and can only benefit the players at the top.

The next thing to follow will be hyper inflation , and that our country will most likely experience a similar situation that involved Germany back in the 1920's, or the US in the 1930's. A depression and monetary devaluation is caused by , the mismanagement of world leaders using blue collar workers for their greedy motives. This will lead to further civil strife ,panic , unrest , and hording that will not cause anything to take place except for the eventuality of a government led totalitarian society. Who ever the leading administration is will be running the show if it is someone like the current US leader it could develop into who knows what, but it would not be pretty folks.

The next big thing on the agenda is the hostility between the US / England / Israel and Iran. World leaders / traders are betting with the use of media generated public charts on a war . This is done under the mentality of politically motivated theology that would, as they are hoping for to stimulate a war with what they see as a adversary that is as dumb as Sadam Husane. This would serve their strategic world dominance game they are caught up in, for great investment return prospects that the generation of wars always produce. If the leader of Iran wants to help them then his continued rhetoric along with his arrogant attitude will make this possible. It is certainly what these world leaders want , if he thinks they are intimidated by his rhetoric then he really is as stupid as they are hoping for .

They have enough nuclear and hi tech satellite tracking equipment to wipe Iran off the surface a 100 times over and they would love to use it , and they don't care what the world would say about it , because they don't need to live in the US , besides all their personal wealth is in off shore or non US bank's. World dominance has become a high stake's game for such people , we have seen this in the present administration.

Chapter 18 Training system failure

There is no shortage of jobs for people that have a education or
technical background in just about every industry that is in the U.S..
This was the main Idea of what the big company's were getting at
when they out sourced all the low tech manufacturing, the problem
is no body trained anybody to do these jobs. The high tech
managers , did not concern them selves with this because there was
this thriving of quick money that captured their attention , and then
the government cut all the program's for some reason , probably to
cover there broke ass's for all the failed plan's and financial
blunders that went on , and in conjunction with a culture that had
chosen to ignore the requirements needed to for fill there own
contract's they were awarded billion's of dollars for.

If everybody is preoccupied with taking money who's going to
make sure the work can be accomplished , well I guess it was the
same people that were going to make sure that sub-prime mortgages
would be paid ,on over priced cheap housing. What a scam , I call
it the crime of the century .

I will explain it in a elaborated text of a specific subject matter.

Example # 1.   Aerospace manufacturing companies

The reason I choose this subject is because it sums up the pinnacle
of technical manufacturing achievement / bulk of the high end
money products produced in the U.S. and that the rest of the world
for the most part has relied on U.S. built aircraft to sustain their
required equipment needs at a affordable price particularly in the
used aircraft market where in the rest of the world in particular the
poorer country's , often then not use used American designed and or
manufactured aircraft and then develop their capability, and go on

to utilize or purchase new American designed / made aircraft, Airplane's , Jet's , and Helicopter's.

The construction of aircraft and most all of the required sub-component's or assemblies required for final assy , are and were always accomplished by a society of manufacture's that had to foster and raise its own educated level and or subculture to enhance and or promote that industry. This must be accomplished with a degree of professionalism , and I would know that because I was raised in such a environment , and active in it for the most part of my life , so I would legitimately understand any aspects that I would comment about, and that I have been recognized by the FAA , so I know a little bit about this subject, however most professions have a similar system and a sub-culture that promotes apprentices and recognized experts in their respective field of their industry society.

Almost all aspects of aircraft must adhere to FAA regulations , inspections , specifications , procedures , licensing , mandatory recurrent certification of licensing for aircraft and or airman that are to be certified for continues un-disrupted and or without incident use in particular respect to do with safety , and the best possible way to enhance and never undermine in active use.

Well this is not so easily and or these days affordably accomplished and on top of that there are a lot of people that would like to work in this industry that do not take it seriously and or they try to manipulate and use it for their personal opinion of use. This is not accepted well, and non productive and or not pro-active in developing safe operating practice's , I was informed by the FAA that there is a big problem getting FAA approved airman licensed in their ability to pass a prescreening drug test. So regardless as to what you would teach someone , if a company had such a program and they cant pass a drug test , they cannot go any further,

182

at that point its like playing monopoly and everybody keeps hitting the go to jail square and the game cannot proceed until they get out of jail after so many try's of having bad luck. The aerospace society of workmen or engineer's must have a more modern and collective view in gaining the work force required to for fill this country's potential , there must be the type of aggressive recruiting method used to gain a work force that would enable the aerospace community to start becoming a proactive force , this would lead to a trickle up affect starting from the bottom up where such things come from , realistically.

This is due to the manufacturing company's having the personnel required to succeed . There are a lot of personnel agency's on the internet these days and they are doing a great and aggressive job at perusing and supplying personnel to the best of their ability , however there must be a supply of workers , they must be supplemented by state run training programs that are non-existent and or under funded to do training , I know because I did contribute to the starting of such a facility , and to this day is still under funded and given only the minimum amount of federal support , required to promote a healthy aerospace training capability, right in the middle of the Los Angeles City Area.

 I would further elaborate on this subject by saying even if you don't hit the go to jail square for using drugs you would hit the go to jail square because your car had its picture taken because you were a split second off on making the light , and you get a ticket that costs $300.00 , now you cant even afford to have a job because your hole life goes down the toilet because you don't have the $300.00 to pay the fine and it becomes a cancer on your life from a financial point, and or a multitude of different other things that will end you up in the jail square. Maybe you need to see the dentist , repair you car , health care , no insurance , The point is people have to be able to live and need to have a reason to think the right way for their own future and not what they have to do that is based on a desperate situation.

This is the main reason any society in any country could not perform , in that it has been made impossible for them to do so financially because the people that work for the government insist that they must be paid to have their job , this being true it cannot be based on squeezing the money out of the people, that is only legalized protection and or corruption.

Most of the things we do in this country on a average are performed in most country's , doctor's , lawyer's , accountant's , federal employee's , computer technician's , the biggest difference is in how much they get paid to how much we get paid in this country to do the same thing.   How long did people in this country think they would be the only game in town before some out of towners came around and set up shop. well folks that's what happen to your low tech jobs and their gone for ever believe me , however there is a bright side , there is a huge deficit in high tech work force capability compared to the current industrial requirement . Meaning if you have a education you get paid more then ever , if you don't the job market is very harsh , and there are too many people to do low tech work and very limited amount's of it since most of it is now produced in another country.

At this point because there are no educated leaders and or supervisors with the capability to instruct , that would enable multimillion dollar corporation's to use the surplus of non working unskilled worker's. This problem is from to many people learning how to build houses , and not aerospace products. There is a big difference in financial value that should be dealt with if this country is going to get back on its feet , the people can be retrained but that is a whole different way of doing things then what the past eight years of the current administration has been emphasizing.

Why do you think they have so many people that are working so cheaply , in China and India , they are the richest countries in the world manufacturing U.S. designed products for the most part although the rest of the world does buy from them just as much of their specific designs and or products that are culturally specific to various countries, It's because they only pay the people that do the most amount of work $100. a month. However the bigger and richer company's provide better then those workers could provide for them selves other wise, such as adequate housing , health care , guaranteed pension, and the government does not prey on the people to suck the life out of them before they even had a chance at life. The meek are truly inheriting the earth in those country's, or so they have been lately as far as they are concerned. We don't do that in this country and we are killing our own economy because of it.

In where Los Angeles / Beijing and there urban surrounding area's would be of a similar life style level of equality, in respect to their demographically rated similarity's considered by those country's standards.

The main point of the comparison is to show that because of all the costs required of living and tax's in the United States it is impossible to sustain at a balanced positive income vs. expense, with out incurring un-repayable debt. The Idea that the housing market is responsible for all of the United States problems is ridicules. It might be the biggest contributor of any one area , however it is all the other costs that have equally broke the financial back of the people in this country.

The people guilty are not just the banking institutions , they just happen to have the most amount to loose that is considered unrecoverable loss's , and that they might be the least able to control their situational outcome of that.

 However the responsibility falls with in as much to the major corporations , manufactures , importers , tariff substantiated government regulations, controlling regulators of federal programs , policy's , and or administration operation's managers.   In that the latter not having control of the banking system , further it cause's the banking system to not be properly applied. They are interlinked from all the different angle's , and that one cause's the other to aspire or expire , depending on the circumstance's. Regardless of how bad the banking or the major corporation's of product development's become incapacitated, they are all linked globally at this point.

If one country does bad that is dependent on the U.S. it will be affected , but due to the fact that they are all separated by national region's this will cause the other to be recognized for it's

186

difference's to be bad or good , however they are separated and this keeps things floating along with out causing exact similarity's and consequences to the other.

To give a example of that condition would be to understand that the United States is the greatest deregulated country that has the potential to act boldly in capitalization however the negative side to that is , it has the most to loose , when things don't work out because projected goals did not materialize.

There really is not a honest reason why accurate projection's can not be determined in the U.S. , other then dishonesty coming into play and masquerading as ignorance. There have been many elected officials that acted as if what was happening to their situation was a surprise to them , and a shocker in that they had no idea such a thing could have happened right from underneath their professional nose's. Well I am sorry but I know for a fact that such people have been lying about occurrence's that have taken place , history has documented it , proved , on many occasion's , however there a lot of people that have no such knowledge that things were taking place and could not understand how people would do or plan such thing's.

Well the fact is they do every day , all over the world. The leaders in the U.S. current administration have been doing so for 30 years the entire economic game plan gets tossed around like a football and that it can land in anybody's hands , all in all it's played like a game and everybody makes their best attempt at winning and gaining the most amount possible , it's part of the U.S. culture , and competitive drive that many American's are obsessed with. The other great society obsession is to be a recognized cultural occult this is human nature in that we thrive to be a society based culture in that we want to have recognition from our society, in that some of us want others to desire them , there's nothing wrong with that unless there's something wrong with the way such a thing is achieved , and if it is so by taking advantage of others this is not OK , however there are plenty of people that don't have a problem with their conscious and it does not bother them that they would be so selfish. This is a self psychological effect that some people try to work onto others. It is almost impossible to achieve anything that does not have previous ties to action or occurrence's that had taken place , this due to the fact that many people will not recognize certain things unless it becomes popularized first.

Chapter 19 What can be done

The trillion dollar question is just that , but what will get done is the answer, it's always been that way. What will happen is going to amount to what's been done up to now in the recent years , and that has been so predictable it's disgusting to say the least , problem is that's what happens when the people in charge have there way , and it is their show , so what are you going to do. Change the rules that's a good one ,kind of like what's going on now 10-11-08 , the rules did change on everybody , and now everybody has to wake up weather they want to or not.

What goes on now is , big business has to re-evaluate it's structure design , to incorporate a system that ensures capability that is undisturbed and that there is a least possible chance left to failure if a insurance company cannot pay on it's claim's /awards found thru settlement's and or court hearing's , that's a big problem for the company with deep pocket's , than they will have to reach into their own to pay damages. This can only go on a certain amount of time before everybody sues everybody and nobody can collect from a law suite , then there will be a lawsuit against , the suite stating improper or un-realistic payment methods were foreseen in a , corporation and that a merger and or dissolver under a bankruptcy was not valid.

There is so many thing's that will become so complicated if large corporation's don't step up. They are what the banks have to rely on, the government does not know how to build airplanes , ship's , and PowerStation's or anything else , all they can do is print money to save the bank so they can blow it but if the bank is tied in with the insurance company like it is , then it becomes a second problem for the manufacturer. Product liability is mandatory and that even if self backed that only goes so far , things happen , people get killed , die , regardless of the fact if it was the manufacturer's fault or not , and it is at least 50% of the time.

There's only one thing that can be really done to combat this failure of moralistic value's in society , and that is for society to take a proactive attitude towards completion of well thought out, and conscientious plan's that promote the refinement and further perfection of industries and people to seek endeavors that have a beneficial meaning and plan that promotes people to desire such attitudes in pursuing there life's goal's or desire's and or to have goal's or desire's. This is normally done by young people , and they causing a cultural shift and awareness of such a thing and that this shift , must be a beneficial process that would be recognized buy anyone of any age or culture , in that it should be supported for the benefit of the young more than anything because they are the ones that are going to move such a shift in culture and or have it made popular.

Successful , lucrative , that means our advertising entertainment , and most all the different society's need to be aware of such a thing so they can assist to perpetuate it.

Such cultural facilitating is done because there is substance to it , there's no mistaking it , this is why it will be uplifted by young people ,they are going to be the most honest judge ,that's because it has to do them specifically some good , in their youth.

There must be society specific sub-culture work shop's that people can flock to , they have such thing's on a commercial level in the entertainment and arts . In comparison with respect to industrial arts there is next to nothing. This is a big problem because industrial arts are required for the most part to be part of the bulk of society's population use , not to mention that the entertainment art's are dependent on the industrial aspects as well , even it is not considered esthetic to admit to such a thing , that buy the way is a problem that should be considered by the entertainment business they just might find them selves with better trained and more competitive personnel if they could entertain that idea more.

They will in the future because all the new technology is developing into digital transfer of all technology and equipment used for the most part , so it will only be a matter of time until everybody gets up-graded completely . Along with technology being upgraded people need to be mentally up-graded to recognize real worth of their situation and or people that they work with.   The personnel to operate the equipment that is available and considered state of the art , due not satisfy the projection's or demand and that if demand is not met customers will go else where if they have to.

This leads to a further of the under capability of the economy , and other country's making money and not the U.S. When the early Airline company's started operating turbo props and jets they hired and trained mechanics , they also operated FAA approved flight schools , that upon completion there student's would receive employment this is a trade upgrade system that is still in use today with the more successful company's that have a budget for expansion.

These self surviving programs were required for the airline and or air charter so they would have the personnel to operate , and that there was always a requirement because most people were in a journey man situation there for that industry had to be based on a support and or sub-culture for it to keep up with it's self. This would first be thought of as a public relation's aspect, and responsibility, and it is until it gets to the technical end of the work there for a company has to have a full time training and recruiting department in order to sustain and grow as required / planned.

The government needs to put more of a effort towards a subsidized aspect of a commercial operation. If the government would help a apprentice and or subsidized such a program per employer a company would at least have the manned power requirement to grow and or be capable , as to not be caused to stop operation for lack of ground support personnel . If government would do just a little amount to help who should receive it , the benefit would be several times greater , for a lot less spent on giving to the corrupt industries , or corporation's. Just doing that would cause more to be corrected then anything that the banks and financial institution's could ever comprehend.

There is a large amount of equipment that is appropriated for government use , that not always see use or has seen more use then is practical to operate any longer. This goes for real-estate , buildings , property's , that could be appropriated for supplemental training to have a government backed recourse and that if locations were placed within commercial aspects of industry operations taking place , this would serve a useful purpose in training and support that industries need to keep up with them selves.

The government does this there called interns , well I have news for you the industrial arts and education programs need to have such programs of training at collage level interns or apprentices, and as well at younger levels to help other wise distraught situations from taking place instead of creating a concentration of skill development early on in life when it would do the most amount of benefit towards people .

There were many programs when I was younger and growing up in Southern Calif., but I have not seem to many of those programs or government budgets to operate them these days , however they have to be operated or the industry will lag. I have seen first hand that these programs work and that industry does benefit from the described programs. People are compelled to work with each other on a social level , the various programs take that group effect of significance in , and they work and create activity that causes effect's and furtherance of society's.

These programs must be generally understood that they are subject to change in accordance with geographical locations , in that if a resource would require development and or if was no longer applicable in a certain location were a predominant industry does not locally support a training base area. Industrial arts industry's are susceptible to change locations for certain reasons , building's , training resources and or worker recruitment , cost to operate in a given region, these aspects would be part of a factor considered by major industry industrial arts based company's.

There are a lot of collages in the upper east coast area , and that there is also a lot of aerospace manufacturing that takes place there compared to California. There is a reason for everything however if major U.S. city's don't take advantage of the available competitive personnel , it would be furthering it's disassociation from the industrial arts that should be equally balanced for society's to have any type of continuity to take hold and cause a serge in employment and money / tax's earned. We really don't have a choice if the already present imbalance is not corrected it will cause a deficit in diversification in society to take place and we will de-evolve , as ridicules as that sounds it is already happening , (devolution) to society.

That's why the problem must be corrected it is causing great unforeseen event's and that big business can not be made to not be profitable , and in order for that to take place it has to operate efficiently in a financial as well as technical /practical method. Industrialization is what the world is actually based on if anybody cares to remember such a concept , it is why we are here , and it is why there was a capability to have global trading partner's and all the diversification that has a massed the wealth in the world today , it did not come from banks , a bank does not produce anything including money , that comes from the government, and big business.

The world has been caught up in living up to the expectations of banks and credit rating's, we have been overthrown by the object that had gained so much reverence as to it's self worth. The banks were merely false idols that we were warned against by those that were wise and understood , however the people did not want to listen , and that having a party and forgetting about it was more important.

Now it is time to pay the piper and if you do not all the snakes will return and things will continue to be formable and not advantages , living will not be easy and you will have to live in fear for snakes, metaphorically speaking. New ways of creating institution's must prevail. The old ones , are failures and or corrupt. If the people don't get behind a system that they have confidence in , thing's will not become better by them self that's why they are the way they are now , nobody did anything to make it better so it deteriated.

All systems ,organization's , ect have to be maintained for integrity to be continues , other wise it for many different reasons ,in general people will take advantage of a easy prey situation. The integrity of a monitoring systems must not be compromised , it has to prevail or nothing will result except failure and discord.   The officers of enforcement procedures must be accountable for their action's , and need to be the most closely monitored or judged of all , that's because they are considered the example of the proper procedure where guidance inspiration , and chain of authority is striven to achieve.

With out this type of higharcy in our systems, complete chaos is sure to prevail. Young society's must have a substantiated basis to find there inclusion not compromised. They would also find a disincentive circumstance considered a embarrassment to them and the use of their time. This goes to explain and demonstrate that the young people of today have defiantly evolved into their own substantiation in that the older and greed based cultures that cause all the problems have left them with nothing and that they are continually requiring to re-define them selves , in doing this a ability to re-define and adapt has been the method on today's

194

survival , when it comes to dealing with a commercially motivated society. This lends to the mobility to not have their life compromised bythe ignorant and or the greedy / corrupt.   This also promotes creativity in that when forced to re-define and or substantiate topic's those topic's are up-graded and made current in that they are kept competitive by doing so.

This is the basic pro-creative attitude , the basic corrupt attitude is based on deception and or , planning that is not realistic or is meant to undermine the standard's that would further the plans of successful cause's. This is done on the basis of non-mobility and or the deceptive force wanting and or desiring to control and overly monitor in a greed motivated way that only leads to the free thinkers wanting to plan on getting as far as possible from such people that are trying to control them. When everything has been tried, it ends up this way no-matter what, so don't wait, start thinking on your own now, before it's to late.

Chapter 20   Under minded

A double meaning on this chapter title of what is going on in society circle's in as much as there are people that know better , than what they are putting out to be perceived to others, is the mentality to there their purpose's. It seems that there are many among us that want to act as if they are with out knowledge to what they are engaged with, for the purpose of furthering their carrier. They do this to escape responsibility , and or their ineptness , and in many case's to circumvent the quality of their responsibility's in relation to what they are perusing .

This has made people for the most part in a business relation with their spouse , or friend's , and that people are going to get into a relationship or financially get them selves out of a relationship based on their financial status and or the person they are doing business with and or their spouse's. They have sacrificed their life's ambition's , their children's , all for the sake of money , and its associated purpose's.

This is effecting people in every form of endeavor and is not at all natural ,and the only thing that is being promoted from such idea's is corruption. The basis of the current government administration has left it in complete disorder , with investigation's and many of our government leaders being brought up on corruption charges.

There has never been a abuse of power this widespread since the US declared it's independence from England because of a similar situation that was taking place back then. If our leaders don't start taking a good look at why the results of this administration have to be made as to not have repeated scenario's there will not be anything left of our system that operated under integrity.
There is no amount of money that can fix a cultural failure , it is so

complex when it gets
to that point , and it easily becomes overwhelming and uncontrollable. It is not just a matter of thing's not being profitable , it
gets to the point that thing's become un-safe , un-reliable , un-
realistic , un-healthy , and mainly problematic.

Cultural failure is what brings country's all the way down , we
could end up similarly to a communist country if we don't stop
acting like one , because that is what's taking place. Very soon the
banks will be run by the government, if were not careful other
vendors of goods will be replaced by government institutions out of
survival and or the requirement to have products produced.

This is not cost effective and will further the debt of this country,
and or such work and or contract's that would have been performed
economically would then be allocated to a inside government circle
that would charge a much higher rate compared to a competitive
bid, they would substantiate this by saying it could not be achieved
any other way. This did happen back in the mid 1980's and there
was a dispute in congress in that the original manufacturer of a
product did not want to release proprietary data to a competitive
vendor for which the government had desired to award a
manufacturing bid to.

The original design and or research was paid for and contracted by
the military to a prime contractor (OAM) for aircraft manufactured.
This OAM used the notion and might have been correct in doing so
that the government was not capable and or being realistic for there
qualification capability to achieve the fabrication process , because
it was particular to the capability of the OAM. The OAM wanted
to fabricate replacement parts and or main component's that were
considered to be more costly because they were out of current
production of such particular parts that were required (older design)

The government argued then that for that reason alone they should
be able to peruse having them fabricated by a alternate company ,

and that besides all that , it is the government's option and it was known , ahead of time that they could exercise that option if required. The problem that had arisen is that the government did not gain the permission to use the proprietary data , even though the government had the right to use it as they do all data that was bought and paid for by the government. This is the only way the government could be assured that they would have a way to support their equipment in the case of a company not being in operation and or parts and equipment that would be considered out of current production. The second problem that arose was because if the government did not have the original data how would they know if it was still viable or if it was superseded by the OAM for safety, upgrading, or if OAM vendors were still in use.

This did not stop the government from wanting to have their way and to the eventually win the case and were allowed to use it, on producing OAM aircraft replacement parts.

Even though the government won it's right to use the data , there was no guaranty the data was still good or that it should be used and or federal standards would be up to date . The other not so good reason for all this is because our government sells or lets other NATO countrys help produce our equipment. The US government sells current and or outdated equipment to foreign countries , and that the US government also sells data that would accompany such aircraft , this being a good reason why the OAM should not want to give up their data , that in fact would be considered trade secret and or trade infringement and or a national security risk, and that once others have witnessed such data they would be able to copy it for their own purposes. We the U.S tax payer and OAM company's put our life into this process, and a ignorant politician did not. There are a lot of good reasons that the OAM has for not wanting to release data , however when it comes to competitive bidding in this country that's where the dilemma is called and all other factors limited , on that basis in that anything could happen, that would be like saying the government was incompetent to handle the data , if that's the case the alternative is that they use there own data which they have in a general way , very non-specific per case by case product , in a lot of situations, however all or most of the specifications used to certify and or fabricate aerospace vehicles and or materials are derived from military specifications in the United States , that includes many civil standards as well that would have their certification based on such military specifications. However there not the same as the OAM more complex design aspects.

The main point on this topic is that the government can and will do what ever is required to achieve there goals , regardless as to who approves of it or who does not. This breeds a position of power that is not necessarily good for what's required and it leads to a company's assumptions that can be misguided and found to be bias for certain individuals and or that wish to have there situation enhanced. This is where the problem comes from it establishes a precedent within the government to make judgments that might be considered a abuse of power, and are in many cases just that.

In many different ways weather it has to do with policy's , or contract award's , or civil right's. Once there is a precedent set that abuse's power then it becomes a trend and it is no secret that the current administration is leaning towards that direction when a tip of the scales is hanging in the balance.

It is very obvious in many society's of life that this is going on , it also turns people against each other who do not share common views concerning such policy's. This is very un-healthy and becomes severely ideologically non-conducive for people to conduct business , or relation's , and or platforms to work from that join many people in corporate and or social endeavors. Once this type of bios study is in place people will become obsessed with it and begin to not concentrate on what really is important and that true importance has been forfeited for idea logic behavior. This for the most part stops things and brings them to a halt , it starts to

199

hinder and discourage true integrity because people begin to get obsessed with the idealism of a subject compared with the subject matter and or real subject meaning.

This has been a main problem with differing views for many generation's , and that what begins at a lower level of understanding escalates to a higher level, and than to a point that the higher up responsibility is also sought to be more the blame for the instigation, this might be true but the higher the level of responsibility the higher the corruption level takes onto the covering up and or the hiding of the truth , this in turn feeds the sub-culture of corruption and that when it becomes profitable for people to cover-up such corruption the idea of corruption alone becomes profitable , at that point it further escalates until you have a situation similar to communism where there is a sense of hopelessness because the people are culturally corrupt due to the fact that the government has burdened there culture with this idealism , and that they no longer are inclined to seek a alternative to the situation.

The United States is slowly becoming more like communism every year and that it wont be long until we have converted completely. This is very unfortunate that the greatest country in the world has had it's capability reduced to a social infrastructure that has become so complacent and demanding that it does not comprehend the way things are meant to take place with a country that was as diverse in it's stand for individuality.

The world does not have a other example to go by , if the U.S. fails the world will fail it has been proven as of October of 2008. There has been a lot of critics of the U.S. policy in how our government is run and rightfully so by other country's , however the leaders of those country's that are critic's, have not learned to separate the people from the government the one thing that the U.S. has done over the years , with view's of critic's from our own government, more so than other country's have done on there own behalf. The citizen's of the U.S. at least the ones with integrity have done so ,

200

maybe not to expected results but at least we have stood up to
our own leaders and called them liars or worst with out fear , and
that some day they will be publicly exposed and that policies will
change because there has been documented history that showed and
proved that wrong thinking and policies will not be tolerated.

The future as there are more people willing to stand up against
domestic un-fairness in this country , will have things that need to
get changed, the guilty need do get exposed , and that there have
been many a good man & women that have paid the ultimate price
for the greed and ignorance that was able to compromise the values
of such people that have worked and fought hard for such thing's.
It is for their memory that we need to prevail and not some
monetary value.   The governments of the world have lots of money
and if they did not they could just print more if it was a emergency
and they needed money because some bank demanded payment.
They don't loose even when they fail that just gives them a reason
to print more money or do some other deal that makes them more
money.

The problem is it does not help the small person and or the poor , or
helpless . So that means only one thing and that if you are poor and
helpless , you better form a sub-culture , the rich people do , that's
how they get all your money. For example: banks are like a
beautiful young lady that knows she is , and she knows she can get
what ever it is that she came for, because she is beautiful and people
want to give her money and status , and fame , and all the things
that she would desire because her talent is her beauty.

Well that's what a bank is , it's a beautiful girl and everybody
gives them there money because they want to gain the eye of the
beauty , or they want to be with her circle of friends that are also
beautiful. Please don't get me wrong I certainly do not have
anything against any beautiful woman that I know of , or that I
would know , for all I know , I am just making a comparative point.
There are a lot of woman that are not naturally beautiful in their

201

body or their mind , and they have had cosmetic surgery , and or they were made to look good when they are really not, and that only lasts so long before harmful effects could take place , and there beauty turns ugly and or worst it becomes toxically laden , or she dies from it.

That's what happened to the Banks of the world in Oct. 2008 , they all had a bad patch of silicon implant's and or botox rejection , and now they have been revealed for what they really are , and its not pretty. The moral of the story is don't go to a cheap plastic surgeon when it comes to taking care of your beauty needs if your main idea in life is to survive and be healthy from having such modifications made to your self that are not natural. The other moral of the story is nobody said it was a safe idea to have a plastic society . There are more morals to the story but I don't want to sound too ridicules , besides if you have read this much so far , you grasp what I imply , from the meanings of the subjects that I am covering.

It is real easy to stop the downward spiral, if people would stop thinking so competitively and tried to be unified in their sub-cultures and industry society's , there would be a melding of Ideas and subjects that would take form at very fast paces, that could never be achieved by being a competitive individual that was going to take on the worlds system on their own.

If we do not embrace the rest of the world for what is its true value / worth than it will not embrace the U.S. and we will be treated as we are treating others. They will use us and cooperation will be minimal on their part, this is not conducive seeing how we are dependent on the worlds supply of resources that we do not produce or have the natural capability to produce.
Our present administration has been conducting itself in a very selfish way towards, giving most all the country's south of our border their way when it comes to just about everything except for the ability to travel back and forth unhindered like they did in a time of war , example WWII , Korean war , during those time's the

borders operated in a way that made it possible for workers that came from Mexico or other country's south of our border to conduct them self's in a orderly way that caused most all the jobs that are accomplished by predominantly Hispanic people.

This was started in a main stream steady flow of capability during world war II , in that a lot of these Hispanic workers were performing skilled job's in the aerospace and national defense manufacturing that woman were not able to perform due to requirement of a stronger build of person that was required to perform such work and or the work force needed , all able men were drafted so this was required. By the way a small build of a male worker was not completely adequate for installing propellers , engine's , landing gear, ect on military Aircraft.

The U.S. government has not done the same proportionally in present civil work places. This has caused a severe imbalance to the working relationship of our different cultures , there is a discordance that prevails and causes severe economic strife between North , central , South America , & Mexico our country's are dependent on the other much like the EU , in Europe and that if a economic realization of at least unilateral condition's does not start taking place the U.S. will suffer every bit as much as the country's south of our border .

The world's economy must have a standardization of ethic's and unity that must stop the civil turmoil that is taking place. It comes from the administrators of all the country's and is causing everyone that was not born into money or won the lottery or by some other 1 in a million chance of being financially well off to suffer in poverty. Now I'll just bet if you asked the billion or so people what they thought of the way they are being ruled they would not agree that their government had the best idea on how to accomplish that with their best interest's. For that matter they don't believe in a other government as well. I for one know for a fact that all government's are just as bad as the next one.

The fact is they all make the same claim in that if things were set up differently there would not be enough money to run the country , this has been exposed as a lie , and a farce as of October of 2008. Apparently the worlds governments / banks don't have a shortage of money when it comes to correcting a problem they have a interest in and they waste no time in doing so , not that it helps anyone but them, for the most part. When it comes time to conducting a properly coordinated military operation or providing disaster relief , and or many of the other coordinated , concise programs requiring budgeting / funding-appropriating, there is not any money to do that or some other under minded excuse to not produce and or manage the program's.

This is the root of the problem they start off by saying they don't have the money lie no. 1 , then they say why do we need to fund the program , and they say the program is wasteful lie no. 2 , after people die and or a problem becomes economically unfeasible they come to the conclusion that something must be done their not sure what that is until they talk to a expert and then they come up with their brilliant idea, that someone has been trying to tell them for the past 40 years that they would not listen to. It just keeps going round and round the same old story with different spin each time to keep it interesting.

The government's of the world are comprised of a after the fact way of looking at things they are the original people that will say I can't fix it if it's not broken, and that often times their interpretation of not being broken is hanging on by a thread and ready to break, or already broken and they don't realize it.   How ever I don't believe that to be true in the upper management of government's because I believe they conduct themselves that way by design. It's all part of their grand scheme of thing's to undermine the public / mass's. As of October of 2008 this is proven and documented history.

If there is anyone that does not understand this , then they have successfully brain-washed you and that you have become one of their follower's. It is not for me to judge anyone and I never would but I will not ignore the truth of what I see with my own eye's. My eye's have been wide open for about 30year's now and I think I have seen enough to be considered a proficient commenter on the subject's I have covered in this book, in that I have had practical experience in the subject's related and have suffered from it financially and physically , and in ways I will not discuss. People were never meant to be so discouraged with how the government's of the world had taken advantage of the very people that made so many sacrifices , so that our leaders could enjoy so much of the work that most people will never see fair compensation for in their life time.

There are laws that hold the public responsible for any slightest infraction , even if it caused a life altering effect to such disadvantaged people that were normally good or upstanding citizens of their community , and that personnel that would be considered federally excepted individuals that had conducted the same infraction's would not be held accountable for any reason in some case's . In that some case's might excuse the gross abuse of power that is wielded by the commanders and chiefs that are suppose to be held to the highest standards are allowed to do what they would determine acceptable and not be liable to any standard's that a lesser class of people would . This whole idea of a culture that allows such thing's to take place unrestricted or liable by law has made the world a very uneasy place, in what I have seen for the past 30 years. I was under the impression when I was younger and naive , that things would get better or evolve into a more acceptable way the world would live with out strife being the major contingent of life , well I guess I must have been foolish to think such a thing was possible. However the present / past administration's of the this country have failed at their job , and made much greater error's in policy decision's than I ever thought possible. My idea's are shared by the million's of people in the world that don't want to live in fear , from their own or other country's government , however this is how those government's retain power , by installing fear into their subject's. They also try to make you believe that there's nothing you can do about it because they say so.

Chapter 21 Deceitful Promises

The nature of corrupt politics' is carved from the new spins of old
problems and or renewed systems and programs that have no real
meaning. When I say they have no meaning , that's because the
topic has a hidden meaning, by design.

If a politician say's he is going to fix the world's problem's you can
take it to the bank that he is a liar. If a politician says he or she is
going to fix anything they are a liar. They are not fixer's , or repair
specialist's , or any other self appointed expert of any kind unless
they got a technical education or degree in a science based art or
equivalent / relevant training for what they profess.

To be acclaimed, in a field of expertise that has a valid society of
contribution to people , and have applied there skill constructively
to help people over come strife, in one way or another must be
logically based with out depending on being some kind of a sales
person , in that to fix something that is no longer useful requires a
fair amount of skill , and that I have not really seen or have herd of
such a thing other than John F. Kennedy & Jimmy Carter in the
past 40 years that I have been aware of , in my life time.

Other than those two there has not been any recorded
development's or achievement's that other president's or their
political party's can attest to. That's not saying much for the
majority of president's that were voted into power . I guess there
has been some bad decision's made over the year's , it could be due
to the wrong people developing and or participating or not in the
political system. Many experts link the current administration to the
era when President Nixon was in power, and that the abuse of
power is similar to the existing political culture that is now active.
The nature of politics and business are pretty much the same , there

is something that needs to be achieved and it takes money to do it , and the expertise of people that are not politician's.
However the politician will take all the credit if something works well , and none of the responsibility if it does not and they will blame the apposing party and say its their fault for any short coming's.

We are at a point in time where people will say anything to get their way or make money with out the consequences being considered. This infectious system of lies has brought down the true meaning of life as it is. Biased media and spin expert's are primarily responsible for this , and that their motivation is rating's that is driven by advertising and that they are the true brain washing expert's that give completeness to the desired outcome's that politician's strive to perpetuate.

This goes for any culture in any country and it is a very big problem , and that it is the main contributor of the dumbing down syndrome otherwise known by me as DDS. Yes DDS is infectious it can turn a otherwise capable normal human being into a complete idiot that would believe anything he was told. There is no pharmaceutical prescription that can alleviate the symptoms or repair the damage , that's because it was subliminally injected into society , and that the only really known cure is to self impose a no fly into my head with your get rich quick ghetto seine BS., and for people and society's to stand in revolt to such insane propaganda.

The present administration's main purpose and goal was self perpetuation of mid-east high dollar investment on a personnel level that not too many people are aware of.. England had been making millions of dollars in the mid east since the early 1900's exploiting Iran for its oil deposit's and taking the bulk of the money from the Iranian's. Upwards of approx. 85% of the profit, this went on in Libya , Iraq, South America , & Mexico. These are the kind of business practice's that were carried out by England / U.S.

In some way's the policy's of greed were responsible for feeding the rhetoric that brought Hitler and the other's , in Italy / Russia to power. There was a mentality of the educated business man that he should exploit the natural recourses of a undeveloped country.

History and the event's that were compiled that led to WWII are known. The Standard oil company of New Jersey had personally fed Nazi Germany all the latest oil refining capability to fuel the Nazi war machine beginning in the 1930's, this being in my opinion the main reason that President Roosevelt used to keep the U.S. out of the European war. The U.S. had German business partners up until 1939 . General Motors was also a big player . I am not saying there is any justification for fanaticism , or the rhetoric that the mentioned dictator's were responsible for , however a cause goes a long way when rallied and fed into young and or corrupt people that want to see their home team win the game.

The power of brainwashing was made into the greatest example of the 20th century buy what Hitler was able to do with it. There was a desperate time in the worlds financial aspect's , especially in Germany and all that was needed , came very easy and that the rhetoric was upheld by desperate people in a desperate time. Once the idea was introduced that certain financial leader's were responsible for the decline of the German people , that was all that was needed along with the fanaticism of Hitler. For that matter it was true. Hitler saw the perfect opportunity and rode it all the way to what had taken place, it was put together by him in his mind and that every part of what a tyrant could possible want, to win the minds of the people was laid out perfectly.

The point is if you give someone the opportunity to take a fast , easy and powerful step and they are corrupt to start with , that's when things happen that should not (Hitler leadership). If you preach one thing and practice another , than the outcome cannot not be certain and or predictable , depending on your outlook , if you are trying to accomplish a bad effect then you have a aim in trying to utilize a bad situation for a greedy cause, as history has demonstrated it sometimes works and lot's of innocent people are sacrificed because of it. In this day and age of instant media coverage of event's one cannot be to careful in trying to keep a explosive situation from developing , because it will very fast and easy. People are looking to blame the people in power that are rich for their problems , and it just might be , that they are responsible, not that it warrant's atrocities being committed however when you have a angry mob and they want to have a lynching there going to have their way.

Possibly before anyone can intervene , the guilty that have been lynched ,turn into martyrs , even if they deserved severe punishment that could not possible do such a tyrant justice , the idea that the superior people would bring them selves down to a common level , invokes such policy's for the un-educated to interpret for their desired relevance.

Things are not as simple as people would like them to be , nor is it desired that they are complex however they are and if conditions are not taken into consideration's by our leaders , who will be the example , what will show by example of a non-hypocritical policy , and or society of peace oriented people. These topics are at the very root of why things happen , or why people would be motivated to do certain things. It was Jesus that said he will install any retribution required, that vengeance would be his, that he came here to cause a lot of trouble between brother's , sister's, and parent's in that the keeping of his rule will be kept as he determined.

A world leaders job is no longer that of a certain stereo typed forceful strong mindless and unforgiving nature of a person , that is the old way and there is no place for this attitude in the worlds future if it is going to keep it's self from destruction. Humanism must be preserved by humans and the judgments of Gods wishs respected. These are the rules like it or not and its not because of any body's opinion other than Gods and basic beneficial social behavior conducive to a society based group of educated people.

Most of the time such a attitude from someone is demonstrated because they might personally be motivated in having such ideals , or that they were coached and instructed that they must uphold such a attitude for the greater good of the people and financial reasons both . Our government officials that are in control and I am not saying it's the president although he does hold quite a bit of power, regardless. I feel he is manipulated to serve the purpose that people in his administration have , that are not in his position of power. This is very similar to the president of a company that is paid $250,000 a year to be in charge and responsible for the running of a corporation , however the stock holders of trusts , banks and investment institutions are the real bread winners and or losers if things don't go as planned. This is the very nature of world business and what is going on in the U.S. predominantly. To think or debate otherwise is ignorant to the truth of what has been going on for a very long time.

 I feel very honored in that I have lived long enough to witness the bringing down of the rich and powerful by their own mechanism, If it was up to me I would not have bailed out anyone , I never got bailed out when I needed or deserved assistance, the only thing that would have happened if there was no bail out is the same thing that is going on , that being the small would sell out to the big , there would be some loss cutting and all the rich people would have to reset the game. The poor don't get a break no matter what ,but when the going gets tuff , the rich and un-deserving take care of their own, wow what a system , can I play how do you get in the club ? It seems to me you have to be born into it , that's how all the current players are participant's for the most part.

I guess you could call it a form of U.S. Royalty , didn't we kick a group of people out of our country that gave us the current language system we use for such tactic's. Well it seems to me that some fall cleaning is in order. Can you spell impeach and or accomplices to the undermining of our country it sure would set a good example of what we do about corruption, and demonstrate to the rest of the world that we do not all believe that unfairness is acceptable in this country.

What do we have to loose , there's not a lot left at this point , it probably would not hurt, at least we would be sending a message or starting a trend. It sure would be a different way of doing things that have not been tried for a while , who knows maybe God might smile down on us and have some pity, because we showed a little back bone , like his son did .

Most people seem to take for granted, as if it mattered that there were miracles performed by a humane being that walked the earth. The miracle is that such a person inspired the world and said to the corrupt ones to stick it. That was the greatest of all miracles that ever had taken place , and that it can never be taken back or rebuked for any amount of money , in the hearts of the ever loving faithful.

That is ever lasting , immortal , and supreme power, and that there has been more sacrifices , wars , deaths , and life giving that had taken place because of what he stood for, than any other cause in the minds of common people, you would think that people wanting to retain world leadership would have the brains to realize that , and harness such power for the purpose of society's well being. Well maybe someday it might happen , probably when the world runs out of other option's, that's normally when people do something correct after the fact, hopefully it will not be ultimately too late.

As far as True Evil is concerned in a metaphor of the concept , let me say this , It is of my opinion that it does exist and it always has. This is not only documented by religion's of various belief's but also by non-bias recorder's of historical event's. It's big impact is on society and that it has the ability to attack a individual's perception's on life and ultimate life goals and then multiply such effects to a entire society.

True Evil is the ultimate used car sales man , it takes what someone does not want , makes it appealing to a un-suspecting individual and than sells it for profit , all the while convincing the buyer he is making a great decision. It is a master at manipulation techniques , it has nothing to do with creating anything , except sorrow , with the exception of one important thing , its own recording of event's.

This is its only redeeming benefit in that a demonstration of what not to do , what is not correct , why ignorance and or abuse should not take place is demonstrated. It is the gate keeper to those event's man made or nature made in origin. Non preparedness of such a force will only lead to destruction , anyone that thinks God will save them in their present life time with out action that was performed at some point should re-think it.

It takes people to save people , or it takes neglect to do the opposite. This is what history has taught us. We have accomplished miracles as a society of God loving individuals, that had stood in the face of ignorance and neglect. Would it be fair to discount the pain and sacrifice of others that worked hard to attain a understanding of true evil so that they and others they cared about would not prevail or sustain.

Who among us has the right to speak for God and say how a miracle would occur by not having such ability or knowledge of any such thing and or that they had never attained to , just because they had a nice opinion of how things should be . This is what fairy tales that are told to young children for entertainment or theatrical effects are made from.

For the God worshiping people of the human race to prevail they must have true respect for each other , and that if this was to occur than they would have a chance at cheating true evil out of victory,

213

and not before. That is how the good fight starts and how to ultimately prevail against True Evil.

Manufactured by Amazon.ca
Acheson, AB